seduced by
bacon

seduced by
bacon

Recipes & Lore About America's Favorite Indulgence

Joanna Pruess *with Bob Lape*

Photographs by Liesa Cole
Lea Wolfe, photo stylist

THE LYONS PRESS
Guilford, Connecticut
An imprint of The Globe Pequot Press

The Lyons Press is an imprint of The Globe Pequot Press

10 9 8 7 6 5 4 3 2 1

Printed in China

Designed by LeAnna Weller Smith

"Song to Bacon" by Roy Blount, Jr. reprinted by permission of International Creative Management, Inc.
Copyright © 1897 by Roy Blount, Jr.

Library of Congress Cataloging-in-Publication Data

Pruess, Joanna.
    Seduced by bacon : recipes & lore about America's favorite indulgence / Joanna Pruess with Bob Lape ;
photographs by Liesa Cole.
        p. cm.
    Includes index.
    ISBN 1-59228-851-0
    1. Cookery (Bacon) 2. Bacon. I. Lape, Bob. II. Title.
TX749.5.P67P78 2006
641.6'64—dc22
                                                                                            2005028655

DEDICATION

For Bob, for being far more than my bacon buddy, an enthusiastic taster,
the source of encouragement, and a caring partner in everything beyond gastronomy.
Thanks for always being there for me.

For Nicole, Ben, and Justin, as always my
greatest source of joy and pride.

contents

Preface

When my editor Ann Treistman asked if I'd like to write a book about bacon, the wheels in my foodie mind immediately flew into high gear. A confirmed bacon lover since childhood, I realized that in recent years I was already cooking it more often as I discovered a growing number of exceptional bacons.

I soon found myself obsessed with thoughts of the crispy-chewy, smoky-sweet treat in every guise. Morning, noon, and night, ideas popped into my mind. The first new dish I created was Seared Scallops on Leeks with Reduced Balsamic Vinegar (page 56). Jamaican Jerked Shrimp, Mushrooms & Tomatoes (page 105) quickly followed.

Coincidentally, many chefs and magazines seem to be focusing on bacon. But people have always loved bacon. Its smell carries us back to comforting times. For me, I'm a child again in a warm kitchen laughing with my siblings, or I'm stabbing at juicy *lardons* in a frisée salad shortly after arriving in Paris. I was barely 21, life was filled with promise, and those succulent morsels were pure temptation.

Bacon's taste is like no other. Caramel and wood fires come to mind. Even vegetarians I asked said that what they miss most in the meat world is that unique taste.

In between Ann's request and when I began writing this book, I got married again and found a kindred spirit in my restaurant critic husband, Bob Lape. As it turned out, he was raised on plenty of bacon back home in Ohio.

I quickly pressed him into the book-writing project by suggesting that, first of all, having had a lengthy association with bacon, he had some informative tales to relate. Second, as a restaurant critic he is exposed to bacon-embellished dishes repeatedly and had already described many of them to me in loving detail (oh, those delectably salty, crunchy morsels!). Finally, his keen tastebuds would be essential in sampling my creations.

When I mentioned my project to friends, most swooned with delight and immediately volunteered cherished recipes, both old and new. Happily, several of those grace these pages. Along the way, I never encountered anyone (except vegetarians) who wasn't willing to sample some of the dishes.

Writing about bacon has been rewarding and a lot of fun. Each new recipe—whether it worked perfectly at first or not—allowed the discovery of ingredients or combinations that marry well with bacon. Very few foods didn't take a shine to it. In pushing the limits, I found that not only does bacon flatter savories, it's an admirable complement to sweets as well. Pecan–Brown Sugar & Bacon Ice Cream (page 166) and my French Apple Tart with Cheddar Cheese Crust & Sweet Brittle Topping (page 168) will hopefully convince you of this.

Along the way, Bob and I discovered lots of delicious bacons and some passionate, savvy people making top-quality products for today's demanding bacon eaters. While our favorites aren't always the same, that hardly matters. There are many different styles and cuts of bacon to seduce you to add style and flavor to your cooking. Bacon is fun food. It makes us happy. I hope you enjoy the recipes and bits of baconry.

Joanna Pruess

The very idea of a book on bacon brought my taste buds to full alert. Genius! How totally obvious! A home run in every sense of the phrase. And the longer you turn over the formidably sensual weight of the project, the better it smells, tastes, and IS.

My ancestors were pork fanciers of the first order, and we ushered in every year of my youth with roast pork and sauerkraut. Bacon is central to life in the Midwest. My first paying "job" at age eight was selling bacon's best partner, farm-fresh eggs, door-to-door in Akron, Ohio. I knew farms and butcher shops—this was before super- was appended to markets—and I'd met a pig or two along my childhood paths. I've witnessed at first hand the stupendous growth of Amish restaurants with their spines of bacon, country hams, and roast loins of pork.

This book has perfumed my life for months. Our home has been smoky with bacon's irresistible aroma and sweet with its power to conjure up delicious recollections of simpler times of yesteryear. Using bacon's succulent, salty crunch to create compelling new taste deposits for our food memory bank has been pure delight. (That's also true because Joanna cooks and I eat.)

Bob Lape

Acknowledgments

For my mother, Harriet Rubens, who instilled a passion for bacon in her five kids by serving a pound-and-a-half of it every morning for breakfast. Always very crisp, always thinly sliced.

For the Kofkes, Sally and Gene, who soldiered through mounds and pounds of bacon, recipes, and tested dishes thereof. Sally, thank you for your time, commitment, and wisdom in all matters bacon. And to Gene, thanks to our bacon bard for his lardy lines (page xii) and insightful comments.

Pam Harding, who applied her editorial skills to this manuscript in various forms, and her husband John for sharing recipes and enthusiasm for this book.

Rick Waln, a permanent and invaluable member of the tasting and editing team.

John Martin Taylor—thank you for your insightful criticism and elegant suggestions for the front of this book. Our discussions helped me get the bacon into my words. Like a kaleidoscope, once the information was shaken up and the unnecessary parts were omitted, everything else made so much more sense.

Marguerite Thomas, for her wonderful memories of Julia Child and M.F.K. Fisher and for reading through the morass of bacon literature.

The Lape clan in Ohio, from those still with us—Bob, Debbie, Alida, and Doug, their spouses and children—to those who have moved on to Bacon Heaven but left us their recipes and wisdom.

Karen Berk, Tom Colicchio, Heidi Cusick-Dickerson, Janet Jussel, John Mariani (another bacon wit), Bill Rice, David Rosengarten, Peg Ryan, Melissa and Brendan Vaughan, Russ Vernon, and all of you who helped in many ways.

Ceci Snyder, MS, RD, Pork Information Bureau.

James Ehler, webmaster, chef, and writer for FoodReference.com.

Kyle and Chad Brown, Veracelle and Chris Hansen, Laura and James Mead, and Leah Kling—eager tasters, testers, and samplers all. Thanks for sharing and caring.

And once more, thank you, Ann Treistman, for asking about bacon. Thanks also to the rest of the team: LeAnna Weller Smith, Chris Mongillo, Jane Crosen, Liesa Cole, Lea Wolfe, Jessie Shiers, and everyone at The Lyons Press.

ODE TO BACON

When we consider bacon, we abstract it from the pig.
We're not involved, whether it was huge or merely big.
A curly tail, attractive feet, a well-proportioned snout,
Are not the things which interest us or that we care about.
For us the pig's the means, while its bacon is the end,
Providing gustatory heights to which we can ascend.

In some countries pigs are used to find elusive truffles;
They search beneath the forest floor with eager sniffs and snuffles.
What a waste of effort to us fervent bacon hounds,
Whose appetite for bacon can be measured in whole pounds.

Bacon's used in many foods, it's truly versatile:
Sausage, sandwiches, or hash, or hors d'oeuvres bacon-style.
It comes in strips or bits, although in England they serve rashers.
It's addictive, often sought by swinish party-crashers.

There's nothing more delicious than fresh pasta with *pancetta*;
And when you've had your fill, there is a chance you will regret a
Lack of self-control which is then obvious in you;
But bacon cancels inhibitions, we all know that's true.

Efumecotte is another form well served in Italy,
Where pairing it with mayonnaise is something you won't see.
In France it's called *poitrine fumé*;
We're well aware they eat it, but with what it's hard to say.

Bacon's irresistible, we'd ban it if we could;
But legislators all agree it's just too goddamn good.

We're savoring many bacons with our friends Bob and Joanna.
Even though we'll overeat, they may decide to plan a
Bacon reengagement for more brilliant savories,
To which we beg, on bended knees, to be invited, please.

—Gene Kofke

Introduction

For many Americans, even a tiny whiff of bacon can conjure up joyful memories of times spent with family and friends in the company of tasty, soul-satisfying food. Whether it's eggs or maple syrup–drenched waffles with crispy slices of bacon to begin the day, a grilled cheese and bacon sandwich or juicy bacon cheeseburger deluxe for lunch, or a hearty stew perfumed with cubes of bacon or fish simply wrapped in it and grilled, the juxtaposition of salty, sweet, smoky, and ever-so-slightly bitter tastes tantalize our tastebuds.

Its aroma is powerful enough to lure me out of bed in the morning or draw me into eateries both humble or haute. The moment I hear that sizzle in the pan or even read about bacon on a menu, my senses are aroused. There is also that enticing play of the firmer, meatier streaks against the softer, juicier parts in each strip. The effects linger long after the last slice is eaten. And I am not alone.

Virtually no other food in the American diet is so beloved and occupies as unique a position as bacon. Its salty-smoky flavor, often perfumed with molasses or brown sugar, is essential to numerous regional dishes, from Southern grits and greens to Boston's clam chowder and baked beans. And the famous Cobb salad, created at the Brown Derby in Hollywood, California? It just wouldn't be the same without bacon.

The toothsome texture provides a crunchy foil to cheese, vegetables, fish, and even fruit, as it so admirably does with its classic partner, the tomato, in a BLT. A final garnish of crushed peanut brittle and bacon on the French Apple Tart on page 168 turns this dessert into a magical standout. No, it's not weird. The wonderfully nutty, caramelized, smoky bits perfectly accent the tangy-sweet fruit. If you are bored with just salt and pepper on your steak or baked potato, a shower of crumbled bacon will enhance it.

Bacon is far more than a food. It is a happy state of mind. It excites people to the point where some aficionados liken it to illicit pleasures. Can it be a religion? Devoted subscribers to the Bacon of the Month Club might say "yes." Even vegetarians and people who don't eat bacon for religious reasons think lusty thoughts about it. And consider the rise of alternative bacons from turkey to vegetarian versions that are now available.

In recent years, when most animal fats were considered dietary taboos, bacon was still a permissible treat. With time and newer diets that endorse more proteins than carbohydrates, and coupled with Americans' search for more intense flavors and artisanal-quality foods, the tides have changed for bacon. The focus on low-carbohydrate diets certainly helped.

While there is no denying that uncooked bacon has a lot of fat—the optimal ratio is at least equal parts fat to meat—that fat is the very thing that gives bacon its taste. When it melts, it also makes bacon strips crisp and crunchy. (To my way of thinking, all-lean bacon is an oxymoron; it's a slice of leathery ham.) Once cooked, two slices have only 86 calories and 6 grams of fat, as well as 5 grams of protein and 90 milligrams of potassium.

And after bacon has been cooked in a skillet, why not fry your eggs in that wonderful fat? It's healthier than some margarines, has less saturated fat than butter, and your eggs will be delicious. But so will your croutons for a salad or a chicken breast sautéed in it.

Although 71 percent of bacon is still eaten for breakfast and brunch, it has recently stepped into the limelight (belatedly, some would say) as a culinary superstar. Led by a charge from creative cooks and chefs, many of whom are working closely with conscientious farmers and artisanal suppliers, bacon is in the forefront of food news. This once humble staple now stars in dishes that are served at all hours of the day and evening at some of the finest restaurants. Home cooks can buy exceptional bacons at their markets, specialty food stores, and online (see Suppliers of Fine Specialty Bacons on page 173).

Ounce for ounce, slice per slice, no other quintessential American ingredient has the seductive powers of bacon.

And it has long been so in America.

When the first wave of English settlers arrived in the 1600s, hogs already roamed this land. The Missouri Agriculture Statistics Service writes that on the insistence of Queen Isabella, Christopher Columbus took eight pigs on his voyage to Cuba in 1493. But it is Hernando de Soto who could be dubbed "the father of the American pork industry." He landed with America's first 13 pigs at Tampa Bay, Florida, in 1539, having taken some of Columbus' porkers from Cuba.

The Indians reportedly became very fond of the taste of pork, resulting in some of the worst attacks on the de Soto expedition. By the time of de Soto's death three years later, his pig herd had grown to 700 head, not including the ones his troops had consumed, those that ran away and became wild pigs (and the ancestors of today's feral pigs or razorbacks), and those given to the Indians to keep the peace.

The pork industry in America had begun. Pig production spread throughout the new country. Hernando Cortez introduced hogs to New Mexico in 1600, and Sir Walter Raleigh brought sows to Jamestown Colony in 1607. Semi-wild pigs conducted such rampages in New York colonists' grain fields that every owned pig that was 14 inches high had to have a ring in its nose. On Manhattan Island, a long, solid wall was constructed on the northern edge of the colony to control roaming herds of pigs. This area is now known as Wall Street.

Among the provisions the early colonists brought with them was bacon. In England, until well into the 16th century, the term *bacon*, or *bacoun*, referred to all pork in general. Early continental dialects also used words like the French *bako*, Germanic *bakkon*, or the Old Teutonic *backe* for smoked pork, although they seemingly referred to the back of the pig, the part commonly used to make leaner European-style bacon.

By Colonial times, bacon already referred to the cured sides, backs, or bellies of hogs. In America, it specifically meant the meat between the pig's fifth rib and hipbone. (Today, some Europeans still refer to one half of a fattened pig as bacon. And English back bacon is still far leaner than American bacon.)

Pork was an important early American staple, and once the hogs were slaughtered—usually in late fall—the meat had to be preserved or cured to supply food, often for the rest of the year. As the country grew, bacon provided nourishment for the long periods when no fresh meat was available. The pioneers who trekked West in covered wagons carried bacon. And soldiers on both sides in the Civil War similarly relied on the cured-smoked meat as a provision.

Over time, the two methods used to cure pork have not changed much.

Dry-curing is the oldest technique of preserving meat. The Chinese were already salting pork two centuries before the Christian era. In the first century A.D., the Roman epicure Apicius described the process in his cookbook: the pork was salted for seventeen days, then air-dried for two days, and finally smoked for two more days.

The second method is a **wet-cure**, where pork is soaked in brine for two to three days and then hung for about two weeks. Along the way, early Americans added maple syrup, honey, or sugar to the liquid to impart sweetness to the meat.

Today's artisanal bacon producers essentially use those same methods. In dry-curing, the meat is rubbed with a salt-sugar-spice mixture over several days and hung for two weeks. Flavors really intensify over that time. Several suppliers also crust their bacon with cracked black pepper.

The salt used in curing bacon removes moisture from the meat, while the naturally occurring or synthetic nitrites added to it help retard botulism and other bacteria that require moisture to live and grow. They also keep the meat rosy colored.

While a lot has been written about nitrates and nitrites (over time the former converts to the latter due to a chemical process) and their potentially negative effects on the body, most scientists suggest that the benefits far outweigh the negatives. Some of today's artisanal bacon manufacturers use celery juice, a natural source of nitrites with the same beneficial effects. Bacon that is all natural and nitrite free tends to look gray in color.

Finally, some bacon is smoked over wood in an open chimney. It can be cold-smoked over a low fire for days or up to a few weeks, or hot-smoked with a much higher heat for less time. Several different woods, including hickory, apple, cherry, mesquite, and oak, can be used to impart distinct tastes. (While bacon is always cured, it isn't always smoked; neither Italian *pancetta* nor French *ventrèche* is smoked.)

Making great bacon is only in small part scientific. It starts with choosing the right breed of animal and feeding it correctly to achieve the optimal weight. The rest is an art form with several variables. They include the choice between dry and wet curing methods and the length of time for this step, the blend of seasonings and how much of each ingredient to use, and finally the decision to smoke or not over which kind of wood and the temperature at which it's done.

Mass-produced hogs are bred leaner than they once were for today's fat-phobic consumers. As anyone who has tried to cook a pork chop or roast according to an older recipe knows, this sadly makes for tough, dry meat. The same holds true with bacon. Bacon needs fat for flavor.

Modern production plants also tend to short-circuit traditional, time-consuming methods for making bacon. Brining is done by injecting liquid into the meat, rather than soaking it. When water is added quickly, the meat can't absorb it as well as when it's done over time. So what happens when you fry the bacon? That liquid flows into the pan and splatters all over the stovetop. Of course, the slice shrinks. Smoking can also be done within hours through chemicals and modern technology. Obviously, the quality is not as high as that of handmade bacon.

So given a choice, of course I would choose artisanal bacon. But I really love all kinds of bacon and continuously order dishes with what I am sure is commercial bacon. One very sophisticated friend of mine, Peabody-award-winning National Public Radio journalist Faith Middleton, still holds Oscar Mayer up to all other bacons as her personal standard.

From 2002 to 2007, bacon sales are predicted to grow 15 percent. Clearly, Americans are bringin' home the bacon more than ever in recent years.

HOW TO BUY AND STORE BACON

Bacon is sold pre-sliced as thin, or restaurant sliced (between 28 and 32 slices a pound); regular sliced (16 to 20 slices a pound); and thick sliced (10 to 14 slices a pound). Slab bacon is unsliced and usually has the rind on. It may be cut to whatever size is desired. Center-cut bacon is leaner, and low-sodium bacon has less salt. As long as we're talking about convenience, there is also fully cooked bacon that is heated in a microwave.

STORAGE TIPS

Packaged Bacon: Store in the package in the coldest part of the refrigerator at a temperature between 36° and 40°F. Check the freshness date ("open by" date) on the package. Once the package is opened, use within five to seven days.

Freezing Bacon: Unopened packaged bacon should be stored at 0°F for up to one month. To store smaller amounts, wrap two to six slices tightly in plastic wrap, then store in small freezer bags. Defrost by submerging the freezer bags in cold water for 10 minutes.

HOW TO COOK BACON

There are many ways to cook bacon, and debates about the "right" method abound. After cooking hundreds of pounds of the smoky-crisp treat, the following are my personal conclusions.

Far and away, my favorite way to cook more than a few strips of bacon is to oven-fry it in a large jelly-roll pan or pans with about a ¾-inch lip. Not only can you cook a lot of bacon evenly this way and save time, the rendered bacon fat is more usable, and it saves cleaning a messy, splattered stovetop.

The temperature that I find works best—that is to say, the one that produces the most evenly cooked, straight pieces with minimal shrinkage—is a preheated 400°F oven with the oven racks positioned toward the middle. I line the pans with aluminum foil, shiny-side down, and neatly lay about 12 strips in each. (Okay, the foil's mainly because I'm lazy and it makes cleaning up easier. Actually, it also helps drain the fat from the pan for future use.) I don't think the neatness really makes a difference, but it satisfies my sense of order. Some people like to crumple the foil to get it off the pan, acting as a rack of sorts. However, I don't think the bacon gets crisp enough this way.

I cook the strips for about 11 to 16 minutes, depending on the thickness, until they are golden brown. Not all bacons cook exactly the same, so let your eyes be a guide. Once the bacon begins to render some fat in the pan, after about 5 or 6 minutes, rotate the pan back to front and also move the pieces in the middle to the sides. After another 6 or 7 minutes, exchange the top and bottom pans (if there are two) and continue cooking until the bacon is crisp and browned. Remove strips with tongs, and blot on paper towels. Drain the bacon fat into a heatproof container, cover, and refrigerate for future use.

One tip I learned: If you are making bacon ahead, leave it slightly undercooked and then either leave it in a warm oven or reheat it. This way it won't dry out.

When cooking a couple of pieces of bacon, I pan-fry them, preferably in a cast-iron skillet or at least one that's pretty heavy. Begin cooking the strips in a cold pan over medium–low heat. Once the bacon starts to render its fat, raise the temperature to medium but not any higher.

Unlike bacon in the oven, fried strips should be turned over after a few minutes and also moved around to cook them evenly. A splatter guard to cover the skillet minimizes the possibility of hot fat burning you and keeps the stove somewhat cleaner. They are sold at many cookware and department stores as well as supermarkets. Once ¼ inch of fat accumulates in the pan, drain it off into a clean, heatproof dish. When the bacon strips are browned, after around 15 minutes, remove them with tongs to paper towels and blot dry.

Some people prefer to pan-fry bacon in a little butter or oil. This is most useful either when the combination of butter and bacon embellishes the flavor, as it does in Don Vittorio's Rigatoni with Tomato-Vodka Sauce (page 138), or when sautéing a quantity of aromatic vegetables with a small amount of bacon. If there isn't enough fat, the added oil helps extend the bacon flavor.

To broil bacon, lay the strips in a single layer on a slotted broiler pan and cook them in a preheated broiler about 3 inches from the heat until crisp and brown, about 5 to 7 minutes. They need to be turned and moved around for even cooking. Remove them with tongs and blot on paper towels.

Finally, some people love the convenience of microwaving bacon. Slices are laid between several layers of paper towels and cooked on high for 6 to 8 minutes. The bacon is turned 45 degrees every 2 minutes for even cooking. There is even a wave-like tray in which to cook bacon slices on their side and let the fat run off.

BACONOLOGY

Bacon has its own terminology. Below are some useful terms used in this book and for purchasing and using bacon. Some newer bacon-like products are included.

Bacon: A perfect food to eat alone or to use in everything from snacks to desserts. Or, meat made from the sides, belly, or back of hogs that has been preserved in salt and sugar or pickled in brine and then cured or dried, with or without wood smoke.

Canadian bacon is also known as back bacon or peameal bacon because the whole center-cut loin used to be rolled and coated in ground yellow peas. (Today, if coated at all, cornmeal is typically used.) It comes from the meatier loin rather than the belly. Typically, when sold, it is smoked and fully cooked. It is not really bacon in the accepted sense of the word.

Dry-cured bacon: Pork that is cured by rubbing it with a mixture of salt, sugar, and other flavorings rather than injecting it with brine. The flavors tend to be more intense.

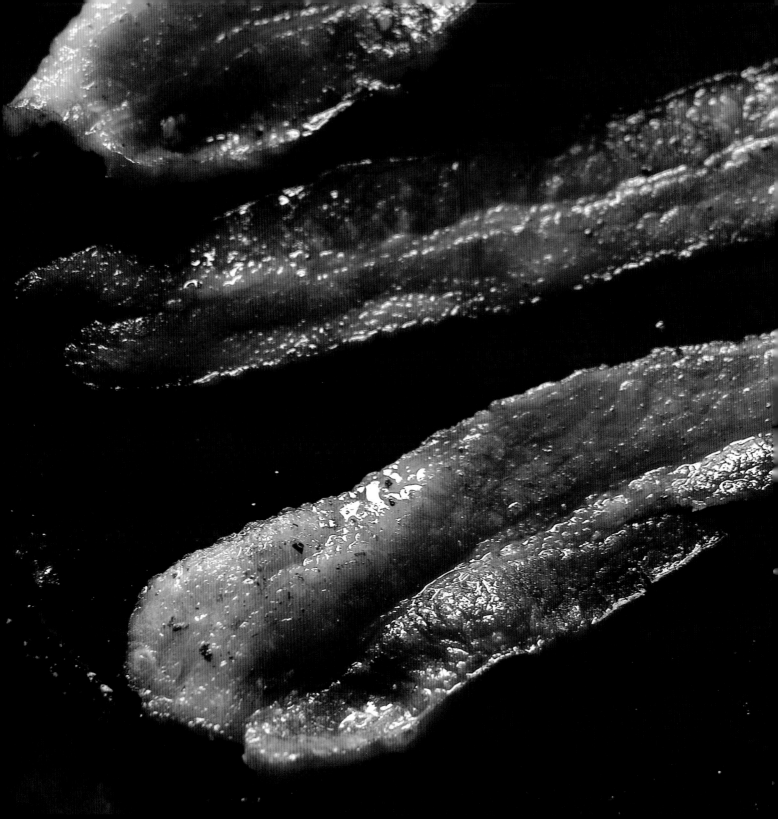

Duck bacon is made from thin strips of the bird's breast that are smoked but not cured. It has about half the fat of pork. Cook it for no more than a minute or two per side. It does not get crisp.

English bacon and **Irish bacon** are essentially the same thing. Both are made from a cured pork loin. Originally the term referred to where the animal was raised: Wiltshire in England and Galway in Ireland were important farming centers. It is leaner than lean American bacon.

Gypsy bacon is boneless pork loin, typically seasoned with paprika and pepper and heavily smoked. It is thinly sliced and very popular with Middle Europeans.

Guanciale is Italian for dry-cured pork jowl. To many chefs, it is the newest bacon star.

Lardo, a dense, white specialty of the northern area of Tuscany, is a much-loved delicacy that looks like bacon without the meaty streaks. It tastes like creamy, bacon-flavored butter.

Lardons: In French, rectangular pieces of unsmoked bacon. They are best when browned on the outside with most of the fat rendered but still moist in the center.

Maple-cured bacon: Pork to which maple syrup is added during the two- to three-day brining period. Honey, molasses, and brown sugar are other common additions.

Pancetta: Unsmoked Italian bacon made from pork belly that is cured with spices and salt, then dried for about three months. It is slightly salty and very flavorful, and is usually found in a sausage-like roll, in a chunk, or thinly sliced. Pancetta is used to flavor pasta dishes, sauces, and stuffings. It is known as *ventrèche* in French.

Prosciutto is aged, dry-cured, spiced Italian ham that is sliced paper thin and served uncooked.

Rasher: English term for a slice of bacon. On some English menus, a "rasher" sometimes also denotes a serving of several slices.

Slab bacon: Bacon sold in a solid piece, usually with the rind still on it.

Smoked, double-smoked bacon: Bacon that is smoked once or twice over wood.

Speck: Produced in the Alto Adige region of northeast Italy and Austria, speck is salted, smoked, and highly seasoned pork. Like prosciutto, it is served very thinly sliced.

Streaky bacon: English term for bacon with a high ratio of meat to fat.

Thick-sliced bacon: about 16 slices to a pound.

Thin-sliced bacon: about 32 slices to a pound.

Turkey bacon: made from turkey breast.

Ventrèche (see pancetta above)

Aluminum foil

Bacon press—a rectangular weight to hold strips of bacon flat while frying.

Bacon wave—a vertical microwave tray that holds up to 12 slices and lets the fat run off.

Cast-iron skillet—excellent for slowly frying bacon.

Glass measuring cups

Heat-proof covered container—to store bacon fat.

Jelly-roll or half sheet pan—a flat aluminum baking tray with about a ¾-inch lip.

Long-handled tongs—better and safer than forks for turning and/or removing hot bacon.

Metal measuring spoons

Paper towels

Splatter guard—indispensable for protecting yourself from hot grease while pan-frying bacon.

Well-insulated potholders and oven mitts

NOTE ABOUT INGREDIENTS

Unless otherwise indicated, please use the following specifications:

Carrots: Peeled

Eggs: Large eggs

Flour: All-purpose

Garlic: Peeled

Lettuce and other greens: Washed and dried

Milk: Whole milk

Onion: Yellow onion, peeled

Oil: Vegetable

Shallots: Peeled

I've long said that if I were about to be executed and were given a choice of my last meal, it would be bacon and eggs. . . . Nothing is quite as intoxicating as the smell of bacon frying in the morning. —JAMES BEARD

breakfast & baked goods

Pecan Waffles with Caramel-Bacon Sauce

Simply to die for! Yummy, crunchy waffles are topped with the most heavenly sauce imaginable: caramel with tiny cubes of crispy bacon stirred in. I like bacon coated with black pepper in this recipe. What a way to start—or end—the day. For a simpler indulgence, just stir cooked bacon into hot maple syrup or purchased caramel sauce to top waffles or pancakes.

FOR THE CARAMEL-BACON SAUCE:

1 cup sugar

¼ cup water

2 tablespoons light corn syrup

1 cup heavy cream

2 tablespoons unsalted butter

1 teaspoon vanilla extract

1 tablespoon dark rum or bourbon (optional)

6 slices thick-sliced bacon, cooked until crisp, blotted on paper towels and finely crumbled

FOR THE WAFFLES:

2 cups sifted flour

1 tablespoon baking powder

1 tablespoon sugar

½ teaspoon salt

⅛ teaspoon cinnamon

3 eggs, separated

1½ cups milk

5 tablespoons melted unsalted butter or oil

1 cup chopped pecans, lightly toasted

Oil to brush on waffle iron

NOTE:

Caramel is made from granulated sugar that is cooked until it melts and becomes a thick, clear liquid. It can vary from golden to deep brown in color. Butter and cream are added to make a sauce. Butterscotch is made with brown sugar and butter. Both love bacon, though caramel works better in this recipe.

MAKE THE CARAMEL-BACON SAUCE:

1. Combine the sugar, water, and corn syrup in a medium-sized, heavy pan. Cook, stirring, over medium–high heat until the sugar is dissolved. Using a pastry brush dipped in cold water, brush down the sides of the pan. Bring the mixture to a boil and cook undisturbed until the sugar begins to turn golden, swirling the pan to color evenly; continue cooking until the sauce becomes a rich amber color.

2. Immediately remove the pan from the heat and carefully stir in the cream; it will sputter and bubble up. Return to heat and bring the sauce back to a boil, then remove and stir with a wooden spoon until smooth. Stir in the butter, vanilla, and rum or bourbon, if using. Add the bacon and serve warm. The sauce will keep, refrigerated, for a couple of weeks. Reheat before serving. Makes about 1¼ cups sauce.

MAKE THE WAFFLES:

3. Heat a waffle iron according to the manufacturer's directions.

4. In a large bowl, sift together the flour, baking powder, sugar, salt, and cinnamon. In a separate bowl, beat the egg yolks, milk, and butter or oil until smooth. Stir in the pecans. Beat the whites until stiff, then fold them into the batter until just blended.

5. Brush the waffle iron with oil. Spoon the batter into each section and cook until the lid can be lifted without sticking and the waffles are crisp and brown. Remove, cut the waffles into quarters, and serve with a generous amount of the caramel-bacon sauce spooned on top.

Bacon-Cheddar Baking Powder Biscuits

**MAKES ABOUT
15 BISCUITS**

1½ cups shredded sharp aged
Cheddar cheese

2¼+ cups flour

2½ teaspoons baking powder

1 tablespoon sugar

½ teaspoon chili powder, hot or mild
according to taste

½ teaspoon salt

4 slices bacon, cooked until crisp,
blotted on paper towels and finely
crumbled

1 tablespoon finely chopped fresh
chives

¼ cup chilled bacon fat

¼ cup chilled unsalted butter, cut into
small cubes

¾ cup milk

1 egg, beaten

Old-fashioned baking powder biscuits get an update when made in the processor with a hint of bacon, chili powder, and Cheddar cheese in the dough. (You can make them by hand, if you prefer.) Serve these warm, flaky biscuits for breakfast or with a hearty stew or soup. They are at their best when just out of the oven. A clean, empty 14½-ounce can of tomatoes with the lid removed works very well as a round cutter if you don't have one.

1. Preheat your oven to 350°F.

2. Pulse the cheese, flour, baking powder, sugar, chili powder, and salt in a food processor until the cheese is well blended. Add the bacon and chives, pulse a couple of times, then add the bacon fat and butter and pulse until the mixture resembles coarse meal.

3. Combine the milk and egg, add to the processor, and pulse until the mixture is moistened and begins to pull together in a ball. Do not over-mix.

4. Turn the dough out on a lightly floured board and knead about 10–15 times, until the mixture no longer sticks to the board, adding a little more flour if needed, then flatten it into a circle about ½ inch thick. Using a sharp 3-inch round cutter, press straight down into the dough. Remove the circles without twisting the dough and place them on an oiled, parchment paper–lined, or non-stick cookie sheet. Bake until the biscuits are risen and golden brown, 20–25 minutes. Remove and serve warm with butter and honey.

NOTE:

When chopping bacon in a food processor, pulse it rather than letting the machine run, to retain a toothsome quality to the bacon. Add it to the machine after other ingredients that need to be finely ground are already processed.

Double Irish Soda Bread

MAKES ONE 8-INCH
ROUND LOAF

In this "double Irish" soda bread, I added chopped cooked Irish bacon to the currants or raisins that are traditionally used in this much-loved treat. Any kind of crisp bacon will add the hint of smoky-salty flavor that nicely complements the dried fruit and bread itself. Serve warm slices of this slightly crumbly textured bread for breakfast, brunch, or afternoon tea. Serve with softened butter and apricot preserves or softened cream cheese and orange marmalade.

4¼–5 cups unbleached flour

1 teaspoon baking soda

1 teaspoon baking powder

1 teaspoon salt

⅓ cup sugar

6 tablespoons (¾ stick) cold unsalted butter, cut into small cubes

¾ cup currants or golden raisins

½ cup finely chopped cooked bacon

2 cups buttermilk

1. Preheat your oven to 350°F. Grease an 8-inch cake pan with bacon drippings or butter; then flour it.

2. Sift together 4¼ cups flour along with the baking soda, baking powder, salt, and sugar into a large bowl.

3. Transfer the dry ingredients to a food processor, add the butter, and pulse until the mixture resembles fine cornmeal. Add the currants and bacon, pulse to blend, then pour in the buttermilk and pulse until the ingredients are moistened and begin to come together. The dough will be sticky. This can also be done by hand in a large bowl.

4. Scrape the dough onto a floured board and knead for about 1–2 minutes, slowly adding more flour until the dough is smooth and no longer sticky.

5. Form the dough into an 8-inch ball and put it in the prepared cake pan, flattening it slightly. With a *very* sharp knife, cut an "X" across the top extending beyond the edges. Bake for 75–80 minutes in the lower third of the oven until the bread has shrunk from the edges of the pan and makes a hollow sound when the loaf is tapped on the bottom.

6. Remove from oven; turn the loaf out of the pan and let it cool on a rack for at least 1 hour. Once *completely* cooled, the bread may be sliced with a serrated knife and toasted, if desired.

IDEA:
Finely chopped bacon and/or blanched bacon lardons can be added to many bread recipes to impart flavor and style.

Rise 'n' Shine Mexican Cornbread

MAKES 9 SQUARES

This spirited cornbread imbued with flavors of Old Mexico or America's Southwest really comes into its own when spread with a mixture of softened butter and honey. Serve it with Blazin' Baked Beans (page 144), chili, soups, stews, or scrambled eggs. Any way you eat it, it's dee-lish.

1. Heat your oven to 400°F. Grease or butter an 8-inch square pan.

2. Cook the bacon until browned and very crisp; remove, blot on paper towels, and crumble. Set aside. Strain the bacon fat into a measuring cup; if needed, add melted butter to measure ¼ cup.

3. Blend the cornmeal, flour, sugar, baking powder, baking soda, and salt in a large bowl. In another bowl, stir together the reserved bacon fat, buttermilk, eggs, corn kernels, bell pepper, cheese, and crumbled bacon. Stir in the dry ingredients until just blended. Scrape the batter into the prepared pan and bake until the cornbread is golden brown and a toothpick inserted in center comes out clean, 25–30 minutes. Remove, let stand 5–10 minutes, then cut into 9 squares and serve warm.

6 slices bacon

Unsalted butter (as needed)

1½ cups yellow cornmeal

½ cup unbleached flour

1½ tablespoons sugar

2 teaspoons baking powder

½ teaspoon baking soda

½ teaspoon salt

1½ cups buttermilk

2 eggs

¾ cup defrosted frozen or drained canned corn kernels

¼ cup finely chopped red bell pepper

1 cup shredded Monterey Jack cheese with jalapeños

 **BACON BITS**

More than 2 billion pounds of bacon are produced in the U.S. every year.

Egg McEnglish Muffin

2 English muffins, split into halves

2 tablespoons unsalted butter, melted

2 eggs, beaten

1 tablespoon milk

1 scallion, including green part, trimmed and finely chopped

Pinch cayenne

Salt and freshly ground black pepper

½ cup shredded Gruyère or Swiss cheese

4 slices bacon, cooked until crisp and blotted on paper towels

A simple but vastly superior version of the breakfast sandwich served by fast-food chains. You can add other ingredients, like minced jalapeño peppers, roasted red bell peppers, black beans, etc., to the eggs. I especially like black pepper–crusted bacon for this sandwich.

1. Toast the English muffins until lightly browned. Brush them lightly with a little of the butter, and keep them warm.

2. Beat the eggs, milk, scallion, cayenne, salt, and pepper together. Heat the remaining butter in a skillet over medium heat and scramble the eggs to desired degree of doneness. Divide the eggs between two muffin halves.

3. Put each muffin with eggs on a square of paper towel or paper napkin. Sprinkle each with shredded cheese, top with two slices of bacon, and cover with remaining muffin half. If desired, wrap in a towel or napkin and heat in the microwave for 30 seconds. Serve immediately.

 BACON BITS

Americans eat an average of four to six slices of bacon at a sitting.

English Muffins: A Tasty Misnomer

You thought English muffins originated in Great Britain, right? Wrong! While explanations about their origins in Victorian kitchens sound oh-so-correct, they're tall tales.

The most popular version says that leftover bread and dough scraps were baked on a hot griddle into round, flat muffins and eaten by the "downstairs" servants. Before serving, the muffins were split so the characteristic nooks and crannies could trap the butter and jam that were liberally spread on them. The story goes that once the "upstairs" family discovered them, the muffins became popular with them as well, especially at teatime.

Yes, it's true that muffins were popular in England during the 19th century and muffin men could be heard in the streets selling their wares from wooden trays slung around their necks. Remember the popular children's nursery rhyme: "Oh, do you know the muffin man?" While tea muffins and the similar-looking scones were eaten, there was not a single so-called English muffin in England.

John Mariani writes in *The Dictionary of American Food & Drink* that when Samuel Bath Thomas emigrated from England in 1875, he brought his mother's teacake recipe with him. In 1880, he began making muffins at his New York bakery, S. B. Thomas Company, on Ninth Avenue. The name English muffin was first printed in 1925.

Today, most store-bought varieties of English muffins derive from Thomas's product. Many British markets even carry English muffins . . . imported from America.

Enlightened Quiche Lorraine

With a single bite of this creamy, custard-filled tart set off by nutty Gruyère and bacon, you'll recall what made us fall in love with quiche Lorraine decades ago. Although I often stir other things into this delicious combination—from asparagus to broccoli and crab to zucchini—the original is still heavenly. My only concession is that I use half-and-half rather than the heavy cream I did in years gone by. The choice is yours.

1 (9-inch) unbaked pie shell, pricked generously on the bottom

2 cups (about 8 ounces) shredded Gruyère or Swiss cheese

1 tablespoon flour

6 slices thick-sliced bacon

1 medium onion, finely diced

4 eggs, beaten

1½ cups light or heavy cream or half-and-half

½ teaspoon salt or to taste

Pinch each ground nutmeg and cayenne

1. Preheat your oven to 450°F. Bake the pie shell on a cookie sheet for 7 minutes. Remove from oven and set aside; reduce the oven temperature to 325°F.

2. Toss the cheese and flour together in a bowl.

3. Cook the bacon in a large skillet until crisp. Remove, blot on paper towels, then crumble the bacon into coarse pieces and scatter it in the bottom of the pie shell. Reserve 2 tablespoons of the fat in the pan.

4. Heat the fat over medium–high heat, stir in the onion, and sauté until pale golden, about 5–6 minutes. Scrape into the bowl with the cheese and flour, toss to blend, and scrape the mixture into the pie shell.

5. Stir the eggs, half-and-half, salt, nutmeg, and cayenne together until blended. Pour into the pie shell and bake in the middle of the oven until a knife inserted near the center comes out clean, about 35–40 minutes. If the crust gets too dark, cover it with aluminum foil. Remove and cool 10–15 minutes before slicing and serving.

IDEA:

Bob's daughter Alida Lape-Peters says she cooks bacon and then freezes it in airtight plastic bags. Her son Kyle eats it straight out of the freezer because it retains its crispiness and there is no moisture, hence no thaw-out time. Now that's a bacon lover for you!

5 tablespoons unsalted butter

1 (1¼-pound) stale brioche loaf

8 eggs

2 cups half-and-half

¼ cup pure maple syrup plus
   additional syrup to serve

2 teaspoons vanilla

½ teaspoon cinnamon

½ teaspoon salt

¾ cup chopped pecans, lightly toasted

½ cup dried cranberries or cherries

12 strips thick-sliced bacon, cooked
   until crisp, blotted on paper towels
   and coarsely chopped

¼ cup confectioners' sugar

Warm maple syrup

NOTE:

French brioche and Jewish challah
are related. Both are light yeast
breads, made with eggs, and great
for breakfast. **Brioche** contains butter
and often has a fetching topknot. It
also comes as a loaf. **Challah** has no
butter and is typically braided.

You can use challah, brioche,
white bread, croissants, and even
baguettes for this recipe. Although
probably too firm-textured for this
recipe, another favorite of mine for
French toast is multigrain bread.

Bacon will always be a willing and
delicious partner.

Brioche French Toast Soufflé with All the Fixins

I simply love this decadent soufflé-like French toast casserole for celebratory weekend brunches. Everything's in this one dish: crunchy bacon, pecans, and tart-sweet dried cranberries are ribboned through the maple syrup–scented cream. I prefer applewood-smoked or maple-cured bacon with black pepper for this recipe, but just about any kind of bacon you like—including turkey bacon—will work. Buy the brioche ahead of time (or buy one on the day-old rack), so the bread is firm. You can also use challah (see note, below). Bacon simply adores the taste of dried fruits!

1. Butter a 3-quart rectangular baking dish with 2 tablespoons of the butter. Preheat your oven to 350°F.

2. Cut the brioche into 1¼-inch cubes. Reserve any bread crumbs and scatter them over the bottom of the baking dish.

3. Combine the eggs, half-and-half, maple syrup, vanilla, cinnamon, and salt in a large bowl and beat until well blended. Add the brioche cubes, turn to coat with the egg mixture, and let stand until the liquid is absorbed, about 10–15 minutes, turning once or twice.

4. Add the pecans, cranberries, and bacon, folding gently to blend. Scrape the mixture into the baking dish, cover with aluminum foil, and bake in the center of the oven for 20 minutes.

5. Meanwhile, melt the remaining 3 tablespoons of butter. Remove the dish from the oven, uncover, pour on the butter, and bake for 15–20 minutes longer, or until the soufflé is golden brown on top and a knife inserted into the center comes out clean.

6. Remove the dish from the oven and let it stand for 5–10 minutes. Sprinkle the soufflé with confectioners' sugar and cut into squares. Serve with additional maple syrup.

Savory Bread Pudding with Canadian Bacon, Wild Mushrooms & Feta

½ cup half-and-half

½ cup milk

3 eggs

1 teaspoon salt or to taste

½ teaspoon white pepper or to taste

3 cups stale firm-textured multigrain bread, torn into 1½-inch cubes

2 tablespoons extra-virgin olive oil

1½ cups sliced wild mushrooms (about 4 ounces)

1 large onion, diced

2 cloves garlic, minced

1 teaspoon dried thyme

5 ounces sliced Canadian bacon, finely chopped (1 cup)

4 ounces feta cheese, crumbled

2 teaspoons chopped fresh tarragon or parsley

⅓ cup grated Parmigiano-Reggiano cheese

NOTE:

Ariane Daguin, a co-owner of D'Artagnan, purveyors of game and fine bacons, suggests that duck or wild boar bacon can be used in exactly the same way as any good bacon—except she believes that it is better and wilder, of course.

She says that duck bacon is best when cooked through to a lardon consistency. Used in a lentil salad with minced shallots and balsamic vinaigrette, it is divine. With eggs piperade it is not bad either.

Here's a surprise: a hearty, savory bread pudding that marries Canadian bacon and wild mushrooms. Any traditional bacon and even duck bacon would be welcome in this mélange. You will need at least eight slices and it should be cooked before it's added. Using multigrain bread brings an extra dimension of texture and taste to this dish. It makes a sophisticated and unique brunch, lunch, or buffet offering.

1. Preheat your oven to 325°F. Butter an 8-inch square baking dish.

2. In a large bowl, beat the half-and-half, milk, eggs, salt, and pepper together until smooth. Add the bread and let stand for 15 minutes to absorb the liquid.

3. Heat the olive oil in a large skillet over medium–high heat. Add the mushrooms, onion, garlic, and thyme and sauté until the onion is lightly browned, 6–7 minutes, stirring or shaking the pan occasionally.

4. Combine the mushroom mixture, Canadian bacon, feta, and tarragon with the bread, gently turning until just blended. Do not over-mix. Scrape into the baking dish and bake for 45 minutes.

5. Remove from oven and sprinkle on the grated cheese; return the dish to the oven and bake until the top is puffed and golden brown, about 15 minutes longer. Remove and let stand for a few minutes before cutting into squares and serving.

Farçon
(Alpine Potato Torte)

If you ski in France's Haute Savoie region, you're likely to find farçon *served at local eateries. Recipes for this hearty potato torte vary from one tiny hamlet to the next, but they generally include bacon and some kind of dried fruit. Serve it warm or let it cool, then cut into slices and reheat in a buttered skillet a day later. The sliced bacon used to line the pan adds a nice decorative touch.*

1. Line the bottom and sides of an oval or round 2-quart gratin dish with the sliced bacon, placing the strips in an overlapping pattern on the bottom and around the sides. Preheat the oven to 300°F. Bring a large kettle of water to a boil.

2. Heat the onion, 1½ tablespoons butter, and the bacon cubes in a large, heavy casserole and sweat the mixture over medium heat for 7–8 minutes, stirring often, until the onions are pale gold and the bacon has rendered some of its fat.

3. In a large bowl, beat the onion mixture, eggs, cream, salt, nutmeg, and pepper together. Stir in the potatoes, apples, and raisins, and scrape the mixture into the prepared pan. Cover with a double layer of aluminum foil and place in a deep pan that holds enough water to come halfway up the side of the farçon.

4. Place the pan on a cookie sheet. Transfer the pans to the oven, pour water into the outside pan, and bake for about 4 hours, or until the moisture is absorbed.

5. Melt the remaining 3 tablespoons of butter. After 3½ hours, remove the foil, pour on the melted butter, and continue cooking until the top of the farçon is crusty and golden brown, 30–45 minutes. Remove from oven and let cool for at least 15 minutes. Invert onto a platter, cut into wedges, and serve.

½ pound thin-sliced bacon, preferably applewood smoked

1 large onion, finely chopped

4½ tablespoons unsalted butter, divided

3 ounces lean slab bacon with rind removed, cut into ¼-inch cubes

2 eggs

½ cup heavy or light cream

1 teaspoon salt or to taste

⅛ teaspoon ground nutmeg

White pepper

2 pounds waxy yellow potatoes, such as Yukon gold or yellow Finn, peeled and coarsely shredded

2 cups dried apples, coarsely chopped

½ cup golden raisins

NOTE:

When lining a pan with bacon where the strips won't be discarded after cooking, use thin-sliced bacon because it cooks through more completely and forms an attractive pattern, as it does with this farçon.

Alsatian Onion & Bacon Tart

½ pound purchased puff pastry, defrosted according to package directions, chilled

2 tablespoons rendered bacon fat or unsalted butter

2 pounds onions, sliced

½ cup homemade or canned low-sodium chicken stock

¼ pound slab bacon with rind removed, cut in ¼-inch cubes

⅓ cup heavy cream

2 eggs

1 teaspoon fresh thyme leaves

Salt and freshly ground black pepper

Alsatian onion tarts are flat like pizzas. Rather than cheese, however, a delectable tangle of golden sautéed onions and bacon is spread over puff pastry and baked. You could also add chopped olives, anchovies, or other savory toppings.

1. Roll the puff pastry on a lightly floured work surface into a rectangle about 8 x 16 inches. Transfer to an ungreased baking sheet and prick the pastry liberally all over with a fork. Cover with plastic wrap and refrigerate until needed. This can be done up to two days ahead.

2. Melt the fat or butter in a large, deep skillet over medium–high heat. Add the onions, lower the heat to medium–low, and sauté until wilted and golden, 12–15 minutes, stirring occasionally. Stir in the chicken broth and continue cooking for 15 minutes, or until the liquid evaporates and the onions are very soft, stirring occasionally.

3. Blanch the bacon cubes in a pot of boiling water for 1 minute; drain, rinse under cold water, and blot dry on paper towels. Heat a non-stick skillet over medium heat. Sauté the bacon until lightly colored, about 2–3 minutes, shaking the pan often; remove with a slotted spoon and stir into the onions.

4. Blend the cream with the eggs and pour over the onions; add the thyme and season to taste with salt and a liberal amount of pepper.

5. Preheat your oven to 375°F.

6. Remove the pastry from the refrigerator. Spread the onion-bacon mixture evenly over the pastry all the way to the edges. Bake in the lower third of the oven until the tart is puffed and golden, about 25–30 minutes. Remove from oven, cut into 8 squares, and serve immediately.

NOTE:

Blanching and/or sautéing bacon cubes or lardons before using them removes some of the fat and salt but leaves most of the flavor to perfume the foods. Once cooked, they remain crisp.

Pork fat rules. —EMERIL LEGASSE

appetizers & snacks

Candied Bacon Bites

4 slices thick-sliced bacon, cooked until crisp and blotted on paper towels

¼ cup sugar

¼ cup dark corn syrup

¼ teaspoon cinnamon

These sweet and savory nibbles, pictured on page xiii, will entice you and bring smiles to anyone who tries them. You might also add a touch of cayenne pepper to enliven the taste.

1. Preheat your oven 325°F. Lay the bacon slices on an aluminum foil–lined baking tray.

2. Combine the sugar, corn syrup, and cinnamon in a microwave-safe bowl. Cook on high until the sugar is melted; or heat in a very small saucepan until the sugar melts. Remove from the heat and brush the mixture liberally on one side of the bacon.

3. Bake for 8–10 minutes, or until the bacon is glazed. Carefully remove and transfer the bacon to a cutting board, glazed side up. Cut the bacon crosswise into squares and serve hot or at room temperature.

Oven-Cooked Bacon in Julia's Kitchen

My friend Marguerite Thomas, a Baltimore syndicated food writer, sent me the following :

Julia Child once invited me and two friends to spend the night at her house in Cambridge on my birthday. We went to dinner on Saturday night, then gathered in our hostess's kitchen the next morning for breakfast.

Julia, efficient and organized, directed us: one person was to monitor the toast, and another set to work making coffee. I was instructed to preheat the oven to 400ºF, and then find a jelly-roll pan in which to cook the bacon. A jelly-roll pan? While I was a fairly good cook, I wasn't much of a baker, and was clueless as to what a jelly-roll pan might be. I was also too insecure to admit it.

I pondered the collection of possibilities in the cabinet that Julia had indicated. Hmmm . . . those round pans seemed like what you might make pizza in, and the flat ones with no sides—weren't those cookiebaking thingies?—wouldn't they work for bacon? No, I guess the grease would run out all over the oven. By default, I figured it out (and as it happened, I did own a jelly-roll pan, I just didn't know that's what it was called). Julia proceeded to lay the bacon strips in the pan in a single layer, but I wasn't off the hook yet.

"Do you mind scrambling the eggs?" Julia said. This was while the others, both more experienced cooks than I, were setting the table, buttering toast, pouring juice, and just generally wasting their culinary skills on menial tasks that should have been assigned to me.

But this time I was more confident, for I remembered something Mary Frances Fisher had once told me: "The secret to scrambled eggs is to cook them very, very slowly," she had said, adding, "It should take about 30 minutes of constant stirring to make perfect eggs." I didn't recall the context in which this bit of advice was imparted, and I had certainly never followed it (with two young kids at home my strategy was always to get the eggs cooked and dished up as rapidly as possible), but I was glad now to remember it.

Did she say to put heavy cream in the eggs? I couldn't remember, but since that seemed like a good idea, I furtively splashed a little cream into the eggs that Julia had already whisked into a froth, and poured it all into the skillet where she'd already melted an enormous lump of butter. I turned the heat to its lowest setting and began stirring. Someone else got the bacon out of the oven and placed each strip on a platter lined with paper towels. I kept stirring. Coffee was poured. The eggs were thickening up nicely. I stirred some more. When the others were all seated I spooned the eggs into a bowl and carried it, fragrant and steaming, to the table. It hadn't taken 30 minutes to cook them—more like 6 or 8—but the eggs tasted fine. "Mmmm, delicious," Julia declared. The bacon was uniformly crisp and flat, not buckled up like mine usually was, and there was no grease splattered across the stovetop. I've oven-cooked bacon ever since, but I've never been able to make scrambled eggs that taste as good as the ones in Julia's kitchen.

Bacon-Wrapped Breadsticks

MAKES 24

12 long, crisp breadsticks broken into 6-inch lengths, such as those made by Stella D'Oro or Alessi or those served at many Italian restaurants

2–3 tablespoons Dijon mustard

¼ cup grated Parmigiano-Reggiano cheese

12 slices thin-sliced smoky bacon, cut in half crosswise

A speedy and addictive hors d'oeuvre, these breadsticks have become a house favorite. There are some wonderful artisanal breadsticks available with different herbs, as well, which would enhance the taste of this crowd-pleaser. Serve with curried mayonnaise (page 43), if desired.

1. Preheat your oven to 350°F. Line a baking pan with parchment.

2. Spread about ¼ teaspoon mustard on each slice of bacon. Sprinkle each with ½ teaspoon cheese, then roll the bacon slice diagonally around a breadstick with the mustard-cheese side inside. Repeat with the remaining breadsticks.

3. Bake for 25–28 minutes, turning once, or until the bacon is crisp and brown. Remove and let cool to room temperature.

Rumaki

My mom used to serve this classic hors d'oeuvre at cocktail parties.

1. Combine the marinade ingredients in a nonreactive bowl.

2. Toss the livers with the marinade. Cover and refrigerate for 30 minutes, then remove the livers from the liquid and pat dry.

3. To assemble, wrap a piece of bacon around a piece of liver and water chestnut and secure with a toothpick.

4. Broil the rumaki in a shallow pan lined with aluminum foil, about 6 inches from the heat, until the bacon is crisp, turning a couple of times, for about 10–12 minutes. Remove from broiler and serve at once.

8 chicken livers, cut in half (about ½ pound)

8 canned water chestnuts, cut in half crosswise

8 slices bacon, cut in half crosswise

MARINADE:

3 tablespoons soy sauce

1 tablespoon medium sherry

1 tablespoon minced fresh gingerroot

1 small scallion, including the green part, peeled and finely chopped

BACON BITS

The expression "bringing home the bacon" is rooted in America's county fairgrounds. Young men raced in circles trying to capture a liberally greased and thoroughly frightened porker. The triumphant pursuer would win the pig and "bring home the bacon." The same fun-and-spill-filled contests gave our language another catch phrase: "as slippery as a greased pig."

Almond-Stuffed Prunes

A tasty hors d'oeuvre with a seductive marriage of salty and sweet tastes.

1. Stuff each prune with an almond; wrap with a slice of bacon, which has been slightly stretched (see note, page 40), and secure with a toothpick.

2. Turn on the broiler and position oven rack about 4" from the heat.

3. Put the prunes on a jelly-roll or other shallow pan and broil until the bacon is crisp, about 5–6 minutes per side, turning once or twice. Remove from oven, let cool for 2–3 minutes on paper towels, take out the toothpicks, and serve.

24 soft pitted prunes
24 roasted almonds
8 slices bacon, cut crosswise in thirds

NOTE:

When wrapping bacon around dried fruits in hors d'oeuvres such as these prunes, the fruit should be soft and pliant rather than leathery. Otherwise, the results can be tough to eat.

1 (5.2-ounce) package Boursin or other herbed cream cheese

1 tablespoon minced shallots

1 tablespoon half-and-half or milk

18 small (2½-inch) jalapeño peppers, washed

9 slices thin-cut, lean bacon, cut in half crosswise

Firecrackers

These hors d'oeuvres have plenty of sparkle but are only mildly explosive. Although jalapeño peppers can be pretty hot, once you scrupulously remove the seeds and membranes, and the chiles are filled with herbed cheese and shallots then wrapped in bacon, much of the heat is tamed. Remember to use rubber gloves when working with hot peppers and don't touch your eyes.

1. Preheat your oven to 250°F.

2. Stir the cheese, shallots, and milk together in a small bowl until smooth.

3. Cut the jalapeños in half lengthwise and remove all seeds and membranes.

4. Put 1 rounded teaspoon of cheese in one half of each pepper and put the other pepper half on top of it. Wrap each pepper with bacon and place on a cookie sheet. If the cheese has become very soft, refrigerate it for 15–30 minutes.

5. Bake until the bacon is crisp and browned, turning often, about 45–50 minutes. Remove, drain on paper towels, and let cool before serving.

 BACON BITS

Bacon sales are predicted to grow 15 percent from 2002 to 2007.

Angels & Devils on Horseback

MAKES 24
HORS D'OEUVRES

24 small to medium fresh oysters, removed from shells, or drained bottled oysters

½ cup dry white wine

1 small clove garlic, minced

2 teaspoons minced flat-leaf parsley

½ teaspoon salt or to taste

Freshly ground black pepper

Tabasco sauce, to taste

6 slices very thin–sliced white sandwich bread, crusts removed and lightly toasted

2 tablespoons unsalted butter, melted

10 strips lean bacon, cut crosswise into thirds

Tiny sprigs watercress

What's the difference between angels and devils on horseback? To aficionados of this time-honored hors d'oeuvre, the addition of a little hot red pepper sauce can transform them from heavenly to hellishly hot tasting, or somewhere in between.

1. In a bowl, combine the oysters, wine, garlic, parsley, salt, and black pepper to taste. Add the Tabasco sauce, if using. Set aside for 10 minutes.

2. Meanwhile, cut the bread into quarters on the diagonal and brush with butter. Put the bread triangles on a serving dish.

3. Line a baking tray with aluminum foil. Position the broiler rack about 4 inches from the heat and turn on the broiler.

4. Wrap a piece of bacon around each oyster (see note below), fastened with a toothpick, and put them on the baking tray. Broil until the bacon is crisp but not burned, then turn and cook the other side for the same length of time. Watch carefully so they do not overcook.

5. Remove from broiler, blot on paper towels, remove toothpicks, and serve immediately on the bread triangles, each garnished with a watercress sprig.

NOTE:
To keep bacon from shrinking while cooking, lay the strips on a flat surface and, using the back of a knife, scrape them lengthwise, then wrap around the oysters.

Cheddar, Bacon, Pecan & Maple-Topped Crackers

MAKES 3 DOZEN
CRACKERS

The blend of Cheddar cheese, maple syrup, and pecans topped with bacon may strike you as unusual. It is—but it's also one of those great, easy hors d'oeuvres to throw together when guests arrive. You can make the mixture and keep it covered in a bowl for two weeks in the refrigerator. It's especially good when served with a little sherry or port. For an open-faced sandwich, spread the cheese mixture on toast and top with strips of crispy smoked bacon.

2 cups (8 ounces) shredded aged sharp Cheddar cheese

2½ ounces chopped pecan pieces

⅓ cup mayonnaise

1 tablespoon real maple syrup

½ teaspoon Worcestershire sauce

36 whole-grain crackers, such as Wheatsworth, Triscuit, etc.

3–4 tablespoons finely crumbled cooked bacon pieces

1. Turn on the broiler and position oven rack about 4" from the heat.

2. Mix the cheese, pecans, mayonnaise, maple syrup, and Worcestershire sauce together in a bowl. Spread rounded teaspoonfuls of the mixture evenly on crackers.

3. Put the crackers on a flat pan or cookie sheet and broil until the cheese is melted and bubbling. Sprinkle on the bacon pieces. Transfer to an attractive plate and serve at once or keep warm in an oven for up to a half hour.

Jumbo Shrimp Wrapped in Bacon with Curried Mayonnaise

MAKES 24

A quick and very tempting hors d'oeuvre. Buy the best-quality shrimps for this, then wrap them in thin-sliced bacon that is slightly stretched lengthwise and secure with a toothpick. The ultimate variety of bacon to use with the shrimp would be applewood smoked. Turkey bacon would also work. I serve it with curried mayonnaise.

½ cup mayonnaise

1 teaspoon hot or medium jarred curry paste, according to taste, or ½ teaspoon curry powder

24 jumbo shrimp, peeled and deveined

24 slices thin-cut, lean bacon

1. Stir the mayonnaise and curry paste together and put in a small serving bowl. Set aside.

2. Wrap each shrimp in a slice of bacon: Starting at the head end, wrap one end of the bacon slice around the shrimp and tuck it under the first turn. Gently pulling each slice lengthwise, wrap the whole shrimp, ending at the tail end and tucking the end of the bacon under the last wrap. Secure the tail end with a toothpick stuck through the bacon and up the center of the shrimp.

3. Set a large cast-iron or other heavy skillet over medium heat. Add the shrimp and cook over medium–high heat until the bacon is crisp and the shrimp are just cooked through, 20–30 minutes, turning the shrimp often to cook all sides. Remove and blot on paper towels. Serve with curried mayonnaise, using the toothpick to dip the shrimp.

NOTE:

The smoky, sweet taste of bacon marries well with the flavor of curry. When the intense but opposite flavors are combined, they excite the tastebuds. Creamy mayonnaise is a wonderful medium with which to blend curry powder or paste, as you can control the intensity of the heat. Try it with Bacon-Wrapped Breadsticks (page 34).

Bacon-Popped Popcorn

The ceramic crock was gray with two dark blue stripes around it and had an accustomed place in the kitchen of my childhood home in Akron, Ohio. It nestled in the corner of a cupboard next to the well-worn Tappan gas range. We called it a stove in those days.

The heavy crock was the repository of bacon drippings. Other than Crisco, leftover bacon and sausage drippings were the medium for frying. I knew it was valuable, but as a boy on the green side of 10, its principal allure to me was that it made popcorn taste good … very good.

At the time when America unknowingly trembled on the brink of a great conflict, my principal conflict was with a popcorn popper. I was intensely interested in the art and science of popcorn making.

Enter bacon fat.

I'm not sure if it was my father or I who first deduced that bacon drippings might be the best way to pop corn. We coated the bottom of a four-quart saucepan with drippings and gently heated it up, checking the state of readiness by dropping in a few kernels of corn, usually an odd number.

Putting a lid on the pan, we waited for the test-pilot corn to pop, counting each explosion. When all had fired off, we whipped off the lid, poured in enough kernels to fully cover the bottom of the pan but only a kernel deep, and replaced the lid.

With the bacon fat in this highly volatile state, the popping commenced and continued as if a thousand gremlins were bursting to get out. It took very little shaking of the pan, but great dispatch in emptying it into a large bowl as soon as the popping started to slacken. There was no trick getting the process underway, but attention had to be paid to stop it before it went too far.

Our goal was to achieve a lid-lifter, enough popped corn to literally raise the "roof" of the pan before any of the kernels started to blacken. With practice, we became adept at lid-lifting.

And the popcorn cooked in the bacon fat had not only the smoky taste of its medium, but also a natural proclivity to cling to salt, to embrace it and make it one with the fluffy morsels.

We learned lessons that remain locked in many years later. We discovered that yellow corn pops bigger than white, and that the best way of all to achieve even salting is to put the popped corn into a large paper bag, add the seasoning, and shake the bag a few times.   —B.L.

BLT Nibbles

These nibbles, pictured on page 30, are a mini, open-faced version of sublime bacon, lettuce, and tomato sandwiches. A single arugula leaf, half a cherry tomato, and a square of bacon sit on crunchy round bacon–Parmesan cheese crackers. The mayo has a touch of parsley, sage, and shallot added. The crackers can be made several days ahead and stored in an airtight tin. The dough may be kept in the refrigerator for at least a week and baked when needed.

MAKE THE CRACKERS:

1. Combine the flour, Parmigiano-Reggiano cheese, sugar, baking powder, salt, and a generous pinch of black pepper in a food processor. Pulse once or twice, add the bacon, and process until the bacon is finely chopped. Add the bacon fat or butter and milk, and process until the mixture pulls together.

2. Remove the dough and roll into a log about 1¼ inches in diameter. Wrap in plastic and chill for 30 minutes.

3. Preheat your oven to 350°F.

4. Remove the dough and slice crosswise into just under ¼-inch-thick slices and bake the crackers on a cookie sheet for 30 minutes. Remove and cool.

MEANWHILE, PREPARE THE FILLING:

5. In a small bowl, blend the mayonnaise, parsley, shallots, and sage. Spread the mixture on the crackers. Add the bacon, arugula, and tomato halves, cut-side down, and serve.

FOR THE CRACKERS:

1 cup flour

¼ cup grated Parmigiano-Reggiano cheese

1 teaspoon sugar

1 teaspoon baking powder

½ teaspoon salt

Freshly ground black pepper

3 slices thick-sliced bacon, cooked until crisp and blotted on paper towels

3 tablespoons bacon fat or unsalted butter

2 tablespoons milk

FOR THE FILLING:

½ cup mayonnaise

2 teaspoons minced flat-leaf parsley

2 teaspoons minced shallots

½ teaspoon minced sage leaf

4 strips thick-sliced bacon, cooked until crisp, blotted on paper towels and cut crosswise into 1-inch pieces

24 unblemished baby arugula leaves with stems removed

12 cherry tomatoes, cut in half

NOTE:

When finely chopping bacon for breads or muffin recipes, add the cooked bacon to the dry ingredients and pulse until the desired size. The bacon will blend more evenly than if you process it first in an empty food processor bowl.

Pizza with Sun-Dried Tomatoes, Broccoli, Onions & Bacon

4 ounces small broccoli florets

Cornmeal

6 strips thick-sliced bacon, cut into 1-inch pieces

8 large cloves garlic, unpeeled

1 pound homemade or purchased pizza dough

12 ounces fresh mozzarella, blotted on paper towels to remove excess moisture and coarsely shredded

½ cup sun-dried tomatoes packed in oil, blotted on paper towels and coarsely chopped

½ medium onion, very thinly sliced

Salt and freshly ground black pepper

1½ ounces (about 20) pitted oil-cured black olives, cut in half

2 tablespoons thinly sliced fresh basil leaves

2 tablespoons drained small capers

½ cup freshly grated Parmigiano-Reggiano cheese

Red pepper flakes to taste (optional)

Pizza is a natural place to showcase any kind of bacon, including turkey and Canadian bacon, and pancetta. This recipe is just a beginning of what you can do with pizza, but I particularly like this combination of ingredients, especially the meatier texture of the thick-sliced bacon. Add red pepper flakes, if you like. I do. To cut basil into thin ribbons, roll several leaves together lengthwise, like a cigarette, then slice them crosswise with a very sharp knife.

1. Blanch the broccoli in boiling salted water until bright green and just tender, 2–3 minutes; drain, shock under cold water, drain again, and set aside.

2. Preheat your oven to 450°F. Sprinkle a little cornmeal on a baking sheet or pizza pan.

3. Put the bacon and garlic in a pan and cook over low heat until the bacon is crisp, remove to paper towels, blot, and set aside. Continue cooking the garlic until very soft. Remove from heat and let cool.

4. Roll the pizza dough on a floured board into a 14-inch circle and transfer it to the prepared baking sheet. Squeeze the roasted garlic from its skins onto the crust and spread the paste evenly. Sprinkle on the mozzarella and add the broccoli florets, tomatoes, and onions. Season to taste with salt and plenty of black pepper. Add the olives, fresh basil, and capers and red pepper flakes, if using, and cover with the grated Parmigiano-Reggiano. Add the bacon and bake until the top is melted and lightly browned, 17–20 minutes. Remove from the oven and let it stand for 5–8 minutes, then cut into wedges and serve.

NOTE:

Cutting bacon into 1-inch pieces *before* cooking will result in relatively uniform pieces to sprinkle on pizzas or wherever you'd like to add cooked bacon.

When the Strip Meets the Slice

Bacon and pizza have a long and honorable history of close association. Fanciers of bacon on delicious discs of baked dough fall into three sometimes-contentious camps:

Some believe bacon should be stand-alone meat on pies modestly adorned with red pizza sauce, mozzarella cheese, and perhaps some decorously sliced mushrooms. Others of more lusty appetite see the crisp strips as the crowning glory of a variety of meat toppings. There is a third contingent that doesn't even contemplate marrying bacon and pizza.

Yet, studies show pepperoni is America's most popular pizza adornment, scoring a point for taste and another for pork products. Unlike pepperoni, bacon brings to bear the intensity of smoky flavor without the spiciness some people eschew while chewing a slice.

Contemporary American pizza makers are powering the new bacon beachhead in the round. What once were thought of as "gourmet" accessories, bacon among them, are now everyday fare, and the ubiquitous golden circles challenge the hamburger as our number-one quickly served food.

There is no end to the combinations, beginning with bacon-and-egg pizzas for breakfast. An Internet search linking the words "bacon" and "pizza" turned up 633,000 sites offering one recipe or many. After reading each and every one, or almost, I can safely report that there are many recurring themes.

BLT pizza and bacon-cheeseburger pizza seem to have universal appeal. But the regional or ethnic influences show impressive growth. Hawaiian pizza links Canadian bacon and pineapple. An Alsatian Onion & Bacon Tart combines bacon, caramelized onion, and cheese on the thinnest of crusts (see page 28). Wisconsin's cheese growers think harmonizing white Cheddar with bacon, walnuts, and sage makes a perfect pie. And many Southern bakers love to pump up BBQ and bacon tastes.

I cheerfully accept the mantle of glutton in reflecting on my favorite pizza. Made at the Washington Depot Pizza Shop in Washington, Connecticut, it was so heavily freighted with meats that I dubbed it "the meatza." The *sine qua non*, however, was crisp bacon, perched atop a welter of meatballs, ham, salami, sausage, and pepperoni.

It was pork times six. The bacon meltdown imbued the crust with the most mouth-watering character imaginable. Could I vouch for the sausage, or meatballs, or even the tangy pepperoni? No, but without the bacon, it simply did not work.

With bacon, it was a taste memory for the ages.

—B.L.

Bocaditos Españoles

Having recently traveled to Barcelona, I was captivated by the vibrant flavors of their cuisine and particularly the many tapas nibbled with drinks. Once home, I combined some of their culinary staples into this fanciful hors d'oeuvre. Manchego cheese, dried cherries, almonds, and smoky Pimentón de la Vera (paprika) are blended with crumbled bacon, a stand-in for Spanish Serrano or Iberian ham for these little mouthfuls.

1. Combine the bacon, Manchego, cream cheese, cherries, almonds, Pimentón, and salt (if desired) in a food processor and pulse until the mixture is blended but not completely smooth. You should still see little bits of the ingredients. Refrigerate until cold.

2. Preheat your oven to 350°F.

3. Roll the mixture into 1-inch balls; put one into each phyllo cup and bake for 10 minutes. Remove, let stand for 5 minutes, and serve warm.

6 slices thick-sliced bacon, cooked until crisp, blotted on paper towels and crumbled

2 cups lightly packed grated Manchego cheese

½ cup cream cheese, softened

½ cup dried tart cherries, chopped

⅓ cup salted and toasted almonds, roughly chopped

1 teaspoon Pimentón de la Vera or other smoked paprika

½ teaspoon salt (optional)

24 purchased phyllo cups, heated

NOTE:

The taste of bacon is more pronounced if it is not chopped until completely smooth.

FOR THE SOUFFLÉS:

Bacon fat or unsalted butter to grease
six 6-ounce soufflé dishes

1½ pounds Yukon gold or other yellow
potatoes, peeled and coarsely
chopped

¼ cup heavy cream

3 tablespoons unsalted butter, at room
temperature, cut into small pieces

5 ounces blue cheese, crumbled

½ cup freshly grated Parmigiano-
Reggiano cheese

6 slices bacon, cooked until crisp,
blotted on paper towels and finely
crumbled

1½ tablespoons snipped fresh chives
+ chives to garnish

3 egg yolks, beaten

1 teaspoon salt or to taste

4 egg whites

Pinch Aleppo or red pepper

FOR THE RED PEPPER COULIS:

2 large red bell peppers, roasted,
peeled, seeds and membranes
removed

2 tablespoons extra-virgin olive oil

1 small clove garlic

Salt and freshly ground black pepper

NOTE:

Aleppo, Syria, was once considered
a great culinary center of the world.
From that town comes Aleppo red
pepper that is intensely rich tasting
but not as biting as cayenne pepper.
It nicely enhances the flavors of
foods with bacon.

Blue Cheese, Bacon & Yukon Gold Potato Soufflés with Red Pepper Coulis

You'll discover a heavenly blend of bacon, blue cheese, and mashed Yukon gold potatoes in these savory soufflés topped with roasted red bell pepper sauce. Using mashed potatoes, rather than béchamel sauce, as a base allows the soufflés to be partially baked and then finished at a high temperature to a puffy height when ready to serve. They can also be reheated.

MAKE THE SOUFFLÉS:

1. Brush the soufflé dishes with the melted bacon fat or butter. Set aside.

2. Meanwhile, put the potatoes in a large pot and cover them with cold water; bring to a boil and cook until tender, then drain well. Return the potatoes to the pot, add the cream, and mash with a potato masher until smooth.

3. Preheat your oven to 275°F.

4. Stir into the potato mixture the butter, blue cheese, Parmesan cheese, bacon, chives, egg yolks, and salt and red pepper until well blended. Beat the egg whites until stiff but not dry, then gently fold them in. Fill the soufflé dishes with the potato mixture, smoothing the tops with a spatula. Bake in the middle of the oven for 8 minutes. Remove and, if preparing ahead of time, let cool, cover, and refrigerate.

MEANWHILE, PREPARE THE COULIS:

5. Combine all the ingredients in the jar of an electric blender and purée until smooth.

6. To finish, remove the soufflés from the refrigerator and return them to room temperature. Preheat your oven to 500°F. Bake for 10–12 minutes or until the soufflés are puffed and golden brown. Remove the soufflés from the oven and drizzle each with a generous spoonful of coulis. Add two 3-inch chives criss-crossed on top of each soufflé and serve.

Potato Pancakes with Foie Gras, Bacon & Apples

SERVES 6

Everyone loves crusty potato pancakes. Topped with silky slices of foie gras, crisp slices of premium bacon, and a sliver of sweetly acidic balsamic-apple sauce, these are a long way from breakfast. As an extravagant first course for a dinner party, it will draw raves. It can easily be doubled.

1. Combine the demi-glace solution, balsamic vinegar, and sugar in a small saucepan, and bring to a boil. Peel, core, and thinly slice 1 apple, and add it to the sauce along with a sprig of thyme. Simmer until the apple is just softened. Keep the sauce warm.

2. Meanwhile, grate the potatoes, the remaining unpeeled ½ apple, and the onion. (You can grate them together in a food processor with a shredding blade.) Transfer the mixture to a bowl, then stir in the parsley, egg, flour, and salt and pepper to taste.

3. Turn oven to warm and place cookie sheet and 6 oven-safe plates in to warm.

4. Pour enough oil into a large, heavy skillet to measure about ½ inch deep. Form the mixture into 6 small pancakes. If the batter seems too moist, add a little more flour. When the fat is hot, about 375°F, add only as many pancakes as will comfortably fit in the pan without crowding, flattening them slightly. Cook until the pancakes are browned and crispy on both sides, turning once, about 2–3 minutes per side. Remove with a slotted spatula, blot on paper towels, and transfer to the cookie sheet in the warm oven. Discard the fat and wipe out the pan.

5. Heat the pan again. Season the foie gras with salt and pepper, and sauté until lightly browned and medium-rare, about 45 seconds per side.

6. Serve potato pancakes on 6 warm plates; add a foie gras medallion and 2 half-slices of bacon on top of each serving. Spoon on apples and sauce, sprinkle with chives, and serve.

2 tablespoons veal demi-glace dissolved in ½ cup water *or* 1 cup canned low-sodium beef stock reduced by half (see note)

4 tablespoons balsamic vinegar

2 tablespoons sugar

1 sprig thyme

1½ tart-sweet red apples, such as Cortland

1 medium baking potato (about ½ pound), peeled

½ small onion, grated

1½ teaspoons minced flat-leaf parsley

½ egg, beaten (1½ tablespoons beaten egg)

2–3+ tablespoons flour

½ teaspoon salt or to taste

Freshly ground white pepper

Oil, for frying

6 (2-ounce) foie gras medallions (see note)

6 slices thick-sliced bacon, cut in half crosswise, cooked until crisp, blotted on paper towels, kept warm

1 tablespoon fresh snipped chives

NOTE:

Demi-glace is available in some specialty food stores and markets. It is often sold in convenient 2-tablespoon containers. It may also be purchased online from www.morethangourmet.com. Foie gras medallions are sold in some specialty food stores and butcher shops. They may also be ordered from D'Artagnan at 1-800-327-8246 or online at www.dartagnan.com. Or, buy 1¼ pounds fresh Grade B foie gras, cleaned and cut into 6 (2-ounce) medallions.

Seared Scallops on Leeks with Reduced Balsamic Vinegar

¾ cup balsamic vinegar

2 slices bacon

3–4 large leeks, washed and trimmed, white and light green parts thinly sliced

2 tablespoons heavy cream

1 teaspoon fresh thyme leaves + 4 tiny sprigs for garnish

Coarse sea salt and freshly ground black pepper

1 tablespoon unsalted butter

4 large diver scallops, tendon removed, blotted on paper towels

This scallop recipe actually inspired this cookbook. Everyone who tasted the dish was enamored by it and asked for more bacon recipes. Seared diver scallops—large sea scallops that are harvested by hand—rest on a bed of thinly sliced leeks sautéed in bacon fat with a touch of cream added. They are topped by reduced balsamic vinegar and crumbled bacon.

1. Pour the balsamic vinegar into a small saucepan and reduce to 3 tablespoons. Set aside.

2. Fry the bacon in a heavy skillet until crisp, remove, blot on paper towels, and chop into small pieces. Discard all but 1 tablespoon of the fat in the pan and heat over medium–high heat. Add the leeks and sauté them until tender and beginning to color, 3–4 minutes, stirring often. Add the cream and thyme leaves and reduce over high heat until the cream coats the leeks, about 1 minute. Season to taste with salt and pepper. Keep warm.

3. Heat the butter in a small, heavy skillet over high heat. Add the scallops and cook until they are a rich brown on one side, about 3 minutes, then turn them and cook the second side for 3 minutes. Season to taste with salt and pepper.

4. Divide the leeks among 4 small plates. Set 1 scallop on each portion of leeks; drizzle with the reduced balsamic vinegar, add some of the crumbled bacon, and garnish each plate with a thyme sprig. Serve at once.

If soup or salad is what you're makin',
jazz it up by addin' bacon. —GENE KOFKE, bacon bard

salads & soups

60

WARM BABY SPINACH SALAD WITH
ORANGES, RED ONIONS & BACON

62

DECONSTRUCTED BLT SALAD

63

PISSENLIT AU LARDONS
(WARM DANDELION & BACON SALAD)

64

SALADE EVELINE WITH LEMON–SHALLOT VINAIGRETTE

67

BROCCOLI SOUP WITH BACON &
CHEDDAR CHEESE CROUTONS

68

SESAME-CRUSTED TUNA SALAD NIÇOISE

70

SWEET POTATO RÖSTI WITH HAZELNUTS,
APRICOTS & BACON ON WATERCRESS

72

ZUPPA CANAVESANA

74

LOBSTER BISQUE

77

CLAM, POTATO & BACON SOUP
WITH KALE

2 navel oranges, washed

6–8 ounces baby spinach leaves, washed and dried

1 small red onion, thinly sliced

8 slices thick-sliced bacon, cut crosswise in 1-inch pieces

2+ tablespoons extra-virgin olive or vegetable oil

2 tablespoons balsamic vinegar

Sea salt and coarsely ground black pepper

Warm Baby Spinach Salad with Oranges, Red Onions & Bacon

I think one of the greatest convenience foods to arrive in supermarkets is washed baby spinach leaves. They and balsamic vinegar help refine this simple classic into an elegant salad to serve for lunch or dinner. Thick-sliced black pepper–crusted bacon is superb here. Remember to toss the spinach with the warm dressing only long enough to barely wilt it.

1. Using a zester or a sharp paring knife, remove the zest from the oranges, avoiding the white pith. If using a knife, cut the zest into thin strips. Set aside.

2. Pare away the pith from the oranges. Remove sections by cutting off a narrow slice at the top and bottom of each orange. Working over a strainer set over a bowl, cut along the membrane of one section and make another cut on the other side of the section, letting the sections fall into the strainer. Continue working until all the sections are removed, then squeeze the oranges to remove all the juice. You should have about 2 tablespoons of juice. Put the oranges in a bowl with the spinach and onion slices.

3. Cook the bacon in a very large, deep skillet until crisp, then remove and blot on paper towels. Discard all but 4 tablespoons of the bacon fat in the pan. (Add olive oil, if needed, to make 4 tablespoons.)

4. Pour the reserved orange juice, the balsamic vinegar, and the remaining 2 tablespoons of olive oil into the skillet; heat just until boiling, then add the spinach, orange segments, and onion slices to the pan and toss quickly to coat evenly with the warm dressing. Season to taste with salt and plenty of black pepper. Divide the salad among the plates and sprinkle with crumbled bacon. Serve warm.

IDEA:

The salad may also be made with arugula leaves, pink grapefruit segments cut in half crosswise, and, after tossing, topped with a little crumbled goat cheese and bacon.

Deconstructed BLT Salad

3 tablesppons extra-virgin olive oil

2 tablespoons sherry vinegar

1 tablespoon Dijon mustard

1 tablespoon mayonnaise

2 tablespoons minced shallots

2–3 tablespoons finely chopped flat-leaf parsley

Salt and coarsely ground black pepper

1 small bunch frisée, trimmed and torn into bite-sized pieces

1 small bunch watercress with coarse stems removed

1 large ripe tomato, cored and diced

2–3 ounces slab bacon with rind removed, cut into 1–1½-inch pieces

2 thick slices country-style bread, cut into large croutons

BLT sandwich lovers: This simple, deconstructed version makes a sensational summertime salad. The usual suspects—some kind of lettuce (I like watercress and frisée), juicy diced seasonal tomatoes, bacon lardons, and croutons brushed with bacon fat—are tossed with a mustard-shallot-parsley vinaigrette with a tablespoon of mayonnaise added. Doesn't a BLT always have mayo?

1. Whisk together the olive oil, vinegar, mustard, and mayonnaise. Stir in the shallots and parsley, season to taste with salt and pepper, and set aside.

2. Combine the frisée and watercress in a large bowl. Add the diced tomato.

3. Cook the bacon in a large skillet over medium-low heat until the pieces are just browned on all sides but still moist in the middle, about 6–7 minutes. Remove, blot on paper towels, then add the bacon to the salad bowl.

4. Discard all but 2 tablespoons of the bacon fat in the skillet. Add the croutons to the skillet and cook them over medium heat until crisp and lightly browned, turning them often. Add them to the salad bowl and toss with the vinaigrette. Taste for salt and pepper and serve at once.

IDEA:

Bacon and avocado are made for each other: creamy and crunchy textures, buttery and smoky tastes. Add avocado to this salad or make a sandwich of the pair.

Pissenlit au Lardons (Warm Dandelion & Bacon Salad)

SERVES 4

I first encountered wilted dandelion and bacon salads in Parisian bistros when I moved there many years ago. I loved how the warm dressing—made with bacon fat and sherry vinegar—tempered the greens' sharp bite. The crisp-moist lardons, rather than the crunchy bacon bits we typically used for our spinach salads, were also a discovery. Sometimes a poached egg was served on top of the salad and tossed before eating.

In French, pissenlit means "wet-the-bed," I think because dandelions were thought to be a powerful diuretic. Their alternate name dent-de-lion, or "lion's tooth," is where we get the name dandelion. It's refreshing to find greens like dandelions and frisée in our markets. People who live in the country can also dig dandelions and sorrel from their lawns in season. All may be used in this salad. I serve it with thin slices of toasted baguette brushed with garlic butter.

1 bunch (about 1 pound) young dandelion leaves, tender sorrel leaves, or mustard greens

4 ounces slab bacon with rind removed, cut into 1- x ½- x ½-inch lardons

1 tablespoon unsalted butter

1½ tablespoons finely chopped shallots

1½–2 tablespoons sherry or red wine vinegar

Pinch sugar

Salt and coarsely ground black pepper

1. Remove the ribs and coarse stems from the dandelion greens; wash and dry them thoroughly (a salad spinner works well). Tear the greens into 2-inch pieces and put them in a large salad bowl.

2. In a large, heavy skillet, sauté the lardons over medium–high heat until the cubes are browned on all sides but still moist in the center, turning often, about 5–6 minutes. Discard all but 1 tablespoon of the bacon fat from the pan.

3. Stir in the butter, add the shallots, and cook until the shallots are translucent, about 1½ minutes, over medium–high heat. Add the vinegar and quickly stir up all the browned bits. Pour the bacon and dressing over the dandelion greens, season to taste with sugar, salt, and pepper, and toss to evenly coat all the leaves. Taste to adjust seasonings, adding additional vinegar, if needed, and serve immediately.

NOTE:

Bacon is often complemented by a judicious touch of vinegar. The sour bite seems to juxtapose and balance those salty and sweet tastes and makes the flavors of the whole dish richer.

Salade Eveline with Lemon-Shallot Vinaigrette

1 head Boston lettuce, washed and torn into pieces

1 Fuji apple or Bosc pear, peeled, if desired, and cut into ½-inch dice

4–6 slices duck bacon, cooked until crisp, blotted on paper towels and finely chopped *or* 1½ ounces finely diced Canadian bacon (see note on page 26)

2 ounces Asiago cheese, cut into matchstick-sized pieces

¼ cup sliced almonds, lightly toasted

2 teaspoons Dijon mustard

2 tablespoons fresh lemon juice

1 teaspoon balsamic vinegar

¼ cup extra-virgin olive oil

¼ cup finely chopped shallots

½ teaspoon finely chopped fresh tarragon leaves

Salt and freshly ground black pepper to taste

Minced duck bacon or even Canadian bacon adds a rich accent to this salad of tender greens, crunchy Fuji apples, toasted almonds, and Asiago cheese. The citrusy vinaigrette makes all the flavors sparkle. It works perfectly with any conventional bacon, as well, but I especially like maple-cured black pepper–crusted bacon for this.

1. Combine the lettuce, apple or pear, bacon, Asiago, and almonds in a large bowl.

2. Whisk together the mustard, lemon juice, and vinegar in a small bowl. Slowly whisk in the olive oil to form an emulsion. Stir in the shallots, tarragon, salt, and pepper. Pour the dressing over the salad, toss to blend, and serve.

 BACON BITS

Bacon is consumed by men and women at an equal rate.

A Serendipitous Salad

Just when you think life is organized, Murphy's Law intrudes. In the case of Salade Eveline, the results were fortuitous.

"No problem," said a foodie friend when I told her I needed my homemade duck prosciutto sliced paper thin for hors d'oeuvres for a dinner party at her house on Manhattan's Upper East Side. "I know a wonderful butcher around the corner," she said, and off we went with the cured duck breast in hand.

When we got there, the butcher categorically refused, saying his slicer would demolish it, looking at the unwrapped object. "Sorry, can't do." A second butcher said no outside food could be cut in his shop.

As despair was setting in, we came upon a ritzy food shop where the owner is known to be difficult. Not seeing him, and egged on by frustration, we entered. Eveline, a charming young French woman at the deli counter, said "no problem" when we explained our request, and took our package. Five minutes later she handed us a neatly wrapped package. Giving her a generous tip for her efforts, we exited euphorically.

Already savoring that first gossamer-thin slice, we tore open the package to find irregularly chopped, ½-inch-thick shards of duck that looked decidedly unappealing. The prosciutto—meant to be a whisper, not an avalanche of taste—was salty and tough when we tried to tear a bite.

With time running out, inspiration fortunately stepped in. The minced prosciutto, tossed with a Fuji apple, almonds, Asiago, and greens, became—*voilà*—Salade Eveline. It was so good, I have made the salad many times with conventional bacon, Canadian bacon, and thick-sliced black pepper–crusted bacon.

Broccoli Soup with Bacon & Cheddar Cheese Croutons

This simple yet fragrant soup takes almost no effort. As an added tempta-tion, thin slices of baguette are brushed with bacon fat and toasted with a shower of shredded Cheddar cheese for divine croutons. The final gar-nish is crumbled bacon sprinkled over each steaming bowl of soup.

MAKE THE SOUP:

1. Cook the bacon in a large, heavy skillet until crisp. Remove the cooked bacon to paper towels, blot, and crumble. Set aside. Reserve 3 teaspoons of fat.

2. Chop the broccoli into coarse pieces. Blanch 6 small broccoli florets and set them aside.

3. Heat 2 teaspoons bacon fat in a large, deep saucepan. Add the onion and sauté over medium heat until soft and golden yellow, 3–4 minutes, stirring often. Stir in the garlic, cook 30 seconds, then add the stock and chopped broccoli; partially cover and boil until tender, about 10–12 minutes.

4. Purée the mixture in the jar of an electric blender or with an immersion blender until smooth. Return it to the pot. Stir in the half-and-half, coriander, and salt and pepper to taste; simmer until hot.

MAKE THE CROUTONS:

5. Lightly brush one side of each baguette slice with the reserved bacon fat. Place the slices fat-side up on a flat baking pan, drizzle with cheese, and broil until the cheese is melted. Serve each bowl of soup garnished with a crouton, a broccoli floret, and some crumbled bacon.

FOR THE SOUP:

4 slices bacon

1½ pounds broccoli, thick stalks and leaves trimmed

1 medium onion, chopped

1 clove garlic, minced

4 cups chicken stock

1 cup half-and-half or light cream

1 teaspoon ground coriander

Salt and white pepper

FOR THE CROUTONS:

6 (¼-inch-thick) slices baguette, lightly toasted

1–2 tablespoons rendered bacon fat or olive oil

¾ cup shredded sharp Cheddar cheese

FOR THE DRESSING:

½ cup Asian fish sauce, available at Asian groceries and some supermarkets

½ cup fresh lime juice

¼ cup toasted sesame oil

4 tablespoons sesame paste (tahini)

4 tablespoons light brown sugar

1 2-inch piece fresh gingerroot

1 stalk lemongrass, trimmed, tough outer leaves removed, roughly chopped

1 large clove garlic

½ jalapeño chile with seeds and membranes removed, coarsley chopped

2 tablespoon each chopped basil and cilantro leaves + coarsely chopped leaves to garnish

FOR THE SALAD:

2 cups arugula, watercress, or field greens, chilled

1 small head frisée or chicory, broken into bites, chilled

⅓ pound sugar-snap peas, strings removed and blanched

8 cherry tomatoes, split

4 slices thick-sliced bacon, cut crosswise into 1-inch pieces, cooked until crisp and blotted on paper towels

1 yellow bell pepper with seeds and membranes removed, cut thinly into lengthwise slices

4 tablespoons each black and white sesame seeds

1–1¼ pounds sushi-grade tuna steaks, about 1¼ inches thick

Salt and freshly ground black pepper

Oil to brush pan

2 scallions, including most of green parts, thinly sliced

1 hard cooked egg, finely chopped

Sesame-Crusted Tuna Salad Niçoise

Black and white sesame seeds add a stylish touch to fresh tuna in this Asian-flavored variation on a Salade Niçoise. Serve it as a main course for lunch or as a light dinner.

MAKE THE DRESSING:

1. Combine the dressing ingredients in the jar of an electric blender and purée until smooth. Pour through a fine strainer into a clean bowl, pressing to extract as much liquid as possible. Set aside.

MAKE THE SALAD:

2. Combine the lettuces, blanched sugar-snap peas, tomatoes, bacon, and sliced pepper in a large bowl.

3. Pour the sesame seeds into a flat dish. Season the tuna with salt and pepper and press into the seeds, covering all sides. Heat a non-stick skillet over medium–high heat and brush it with oil. Sauté the tuna on both sides until medium-rare, turning once, about 2–2½ minutes per side. Remove and set aside.

4. Pour the vinaigrette over the vegetables, toss, and blend well. Divide the salad among 4 plates. Slice the tuna across the grain into ½-inch slices and divide among the plates. Sprinkle on the scallions, chopped basil, cilantro, and hard-cooked egg and serve.

Sweet Potato Rösti with Hazelnuts, Apricots & Bacon on Watercress

SERVES 4

½ pound slab bacon with rind removed, and cut into 1- x ½- x ½-inch pieces, or use thick-sliced bacon cut crosswise into ½-inch pieces

1 pound sweet potatoes, peeled and coarsely shredded

Coarse salt

⅓ cup hazelnuts, skinned and toasted, coarsely chopped + ¼ cup cracked hazelnuts to garnish

2 scallions, including most of green parts, minced + 1 scallion, including green parts, thinly sliced

1 egg, beaten

½ teaspoon salt or to taste

Freshly ground black pepper

3–4 tablespoons bacon fat or vegetable oil

¾ cups canned apricot nectar

⅜ cup hazelnut oil

¼ cup apple cider vinegar

1 tablespoon firmly packed light brown sugar

½ teaspoon each ground cumin and ground coriander

⅛ teaspoon cayenne pepper or to taste

1 large bunch watercress or arugula, coarse stems removed, chilled

½ cup finely chopped dried apricots

A showstopper of a first course pictured on page 58. Actually, I could eat it for any part of a meal because it's so delicious. Rösti are crunchy potato pancakes that are a Swiss specialty. Here they are made with sweet potatoes and hazelnuts and partnered with tangy apricots and salty-smoky bacon in a vibrant warm vinaigrette, then served on a bed of watercress. It's a formidable combination.

1. Cook the bacon in a heavy skillet over medium–high heat until the pieces are browned on all sides, so that most of the fat is rendered but the pieces are still moist inside. Remove and blot the bacon on paper towels. Reserve the bacon fat for frying, if desired.

2. Preheat your oven to 400°F.

3. In a large bowl, cover the shredded sweet potato with water. Sprinkle with a liberal amount of salt and let stand for 5 minutes, then drain and squeeze the potatoes very dry in a clean towel. Wipe out the bowl and return the potatoes to it. Add ⅓ cup hazelnuts, the scallions, egg, salt, and pepper. Blend well, then divide the mixture into 4 equal portions.

4. Heat 2 large non-stick oven-proof skillets over medium–high heat, each containing ½–1 tablespoon bacon fat or oil. Put the 4 portions of rösti mixture in the pans, 2 per pan, flattening them slightly with a spatula. Drizzle on the remaining fat or oil, and bake the röstis in the oven for 30 minutes until they are richly browned and crunchy on the bottom. Remove the pans from the oven and turn the rösti over. Turn off the oven, and return the pans to the oven to keep the rösti warm while preparing the rest of the dish.

5. While the röstis are baking, reduce the apricot nectar by half (this is easily accomplished in a microwave oven on high), then pour it into the jar of an electric blender. Add the hazelnut oil, vinegar, brown sugar, cumin, coriander, cayenne, and ½ teaspoon salt or to taste. Purée until smooth and set aside.

6. Divide the watercress or arugula among 4 large salad plates, laying sprigs around the outer edge of the plate. Put a rösti in the center of each plate. Return the vinaigrette to the skillet along with the bacon, chopped apricots, and the remaining ¼ cup hazelnuts, heat over high heat for 30 seconds, then spoon over the greens and rösti, sprinkle on the remaining scallion, and serve.

1 pound Savoy cabbage, cored and outer leaves discarded

Kosher salt

¾ pound slab bacon with rind removed, cut into ½-inch dice

½ cup extra-virgin olive oil, divided

5 medium–large onions, trimmed, cut in half lengthwise, and thinly sliced

3½–4½ cups chicken or meat stock

Freshly ground pepper

4 cloves garlic, lightly bruised

9 slices Italian or French bread, about 3 ½ x 6 inches each (you may need more or less, depending on size)

5 ounces aged Italian Fontina cheese, coarsely grated (about 1⅓ cups), divided

½ cup finely grated Parmigiano-Reggiano cheese, divided

¼ teaspoon freshly grated nutmeg

Zuppa Canavesana

Sally and Gene Kofke describe eating this main-course soupy dish some years ago in the Val d'Aosta, the far northwestern corner of Italy. They loved it so much that Sally reproduced it back home. It's a little time-consuming to prepare, but really worth it. To serve this as soup, use the larger amount of liquid.

All you need to complete the meal is a salad. (And dessert, of course.)

1. Bring 6 quarts of water to the boil. Separate the cabbage leaves; when the water comes to a boil, add 1 tablespoon kosher salt and the cabbage. Parboil the cabbage 2 minutes or until the leaves are limp. Drain, shock in cold water, blot dry, and cut the leaves in quarters; set aside.

2. Heat the bacon in a sauté pan large enough to hold it and the onions; render some fat but do not brown. Remove the bacon with a slotted spoon and reserve. Add enough olive oil to the pan to make 3 tablespoons of fat, and stir in the onions. Toss the onions over medium–high heat to coat them with fat, then cook over low heat, stirring, until the onion is softened and translucent. Then reduce the heat to very low and cook the onions, stirring occasionally, 30–40 minutes, or until they are a deep golden brown.

3. Add 3½ cups of the broth and scrape up any browned cooking bits on the bottom of the pan. Cover and cook over very low heat for 15 minutes. Season to taste with salt and freshly ground pepper.

4. Meanwhile, cook the garlic in 4 tablespoons of olive oil over medium heat until golden. Discard the garlic. Brush the bread slices with the garlic-scented oil on one side, place them on a baking sheet, and bake until golden and crunchy.

5. Mix together three-quarters of the Fontina and half of the Parmigiano-Reggiano, and reserve for a topping.

6. Preheat your oven to 350°F.

7. To assemble the zuppa, divide the cabbage, bacon, bread, and onion in thirds. Use a large 3½–4-quart ovenproof casserole, at least 4 inches deep. Start with a cabbage layer, then a bacon layer, then a layer of bread sprinkled with salt, several generous grinds of pepper, and a dusting of nutmeg, along with half of the remaining cheeses and finally a third of the onion and broth. Repeat with a second layer. For the third layer, repeat as above, except sprinkle all the reserved cheeses over the bread layer and top with the remaining onion-broth mixture.

8. On top of the stove, bring the liquid to a simmer, then transfer the pot uncovered to the center of the oven and cook for about 1½ hours. Turn the pan front-to-back after an hour, adding more broth if it seems too dry. Cook until a golden crust has formed on top. If the crust begins to burn, cover it with foil. If the casserole was not started on top of stove, you will need an extra half hour of cooking. Serve on warm plates, dividing the crusty top.

NOTE:

Some bacon can be quite salty. Cooking with salt-free chicken stock or low-sodium chicken stock, now widely available, is a good way to control the seasoning. If you do use canned stock with salt, add any additional salt cautiously.

Lobster Bisque

2 (1½-pound) live lobsters

3 large shallots

2 medium ribs celery

2 medium carrots

3 large cloves garlic

4 tablespoons oil

4 slices thick-sliced bacon, coarsely chopped + 4 slices thick-sliced bacon, cut into ¼-inch cubes

1 firm, ripe tomato, coarsely chopped

2 tablespoons chopped fresh tarragon leaves

1 bay leaf

⅓ cup cognac or brandy

½ cup medium sherry

6 cups fish stock or substitute low-sodium chicken broth

½ cup tomato paste

1 cup heavy cream

1 tablespoon unsalted butter

Salt and cayenne pepper

¼ cup thinly slicerd scallions, to garnish

A classic soup that is at its best when smooth as velvet. In this version, crumbled bacon and sliced scallions add a nice counterpoint to the smooth texture and rich taste. Usually this bisque doesn't need additional salt, but add it if you feel it is lacking.

1. Fill a large, deep pot about two-thirds full with salted water and bring to a boil. Add the lobsters one at a time, head first, cover, and boil for 8 minutes. Using long tongs, remove and transfer the lobsters to a large bowl; let stand until they are cool enough to handle.

2. Working over a large bowl to catch all juices, twist off the lobster tails and claws. Reserve the tomalley, if desired; discard the head sacs and any roe. Using a meat pounder or mallet, crack the claws and tails and remove the meat, transfer it to a bowl, cover, and refrigerate. Reserve the shells and lobster bodies.

3. Combine the shallots, celery, carrots, and garlic in a food processor and pulse until fairly finely chopped; do not over-process. Or, finely chop these by hand.

4. Heat the oil and chopped bacon in a large pot or Dutch oven over medium–high heat until hot. Stir in the reserved lobster bodies and shells and cook for 5 minutes, stirring often. Stir in the chopped vegetables and tomato, tarragon, and bay leaf, and cook for 6–7 minutes, until the vegetables soften and begin to color.

5. Turn off the heat. Pour in the cognac and carefully ignite it. When the flames subside, add the sherry, bring to a boil, and cook until the liquid has almost evaporated. Pour in the fish stock, partially cover, and simmer for 1 hour, stirring occasionally.

6. Remove the liquid from the heat and strain it into a large bowl. Discard the thick claw and tail shells. Transfer the remaining softer shells and vegetables to a food processor and process until the vegetables are puréed.

7. Set a large, fine mesh strainer over a medium-sized deep pot. Scrape the lobster-vegetable mixture into the strainer and pour the lobster broth over it, pressing with a wooden spoon to extract as much liquid as possible. Discard the solids. Whisk in the tomato paste, bring the liquid to a boil, and cook until it is reduced to about 3 cups, about 10 minutes. Stir in the cream and simmer 5 minutes.

8. Before serving, cook the remaining cubed bacon until crisp but still moist in the center; blot on paper towels. Chop the reserved lobster into small pieces. Melt the butter in a small skillet over medium–high heat. Stir in the lobster and cook until the meat is just cooked through. Transfer it to the hot bisque. Season to taste with salt and cayenne, then ladle into bowls, add bacon and scallions, and serve.

 **BACON BITS**

Fifty-three percent of U.S. households report that they always have bacon in their fridge.

Clam, Potato & Bacon Soup with Kale

SERVES 6

This zesty soup is accented with garlic, bacon, and jalapeño that play against briny clams and earthy kale. It was inspired by Portuguese caldo verde. But rather than the chorizo typically used for the soup, I like bacon because it's so accessible and marries deliciously with the other flavors of the soup. Serve with toasted slices of French or Italian bread.

1. Combine a quarter of the bacon cubes with jalapeños, onion, and garlic in a large pot, cover, and sweat the mixture over medium heat until the onion is soft, 6–8 minutes. Add the stock, whole potatoes, cabbage, and bay leaves, and bring to a gentle boil. Cook until the potatoes are tender when pierced with a knife, then remove them with a slotted spoon and set them aside to cool.

2. Boil the soup 5 minutes longer, then pour the liquid it through a strainer and set it aside. Discard the vegetables and bacon. You should have about 6 cups of liquid. Wipe out the pan.

3. Shred the potatoes with a box grater or a food processor with the coarse grating blade and set them aside.

4. Add ¼ cup olive oil to the pot and heat over medium–high heat. Add the remaining bacon cubes and cook until browned on all sides, 1–2 minutes, turning them often. Add the clams and broth, cover the pot, and cook until the clams are opened. Remove the clams with a slotted spoon and divide them among 6 heated soup bowls. Discard any clams that don't open.

5. Return the broth to a boil. Stir in the reserved potato, kale, and remaining ¼ cup olive oil. Season with salt and plenty of black pepper, and cook until the kale is tender. Ladle the broth over the clams, add a little additional olive oil to each bowl, and serve at once.

½ pound slab bacon with rind removed, cut into ½-inch cubes

1–2 large jalapeños, seeded, if desired, and chopped

1 onion, chopped

1 head garlic, smashed

2 quarts chicken stock

1 pound baking potatoes, peeled (about 2 medium)

½ head napa cabbage, shredded

2 bay leaves

½+ cup fruity extra-virgin olive oil + additional oil to drizzle on before serving

36 littleneck clams, scrubbed to remove all sand

⅓ pound kale or Swiss chard, thick stems removed, cut crosswise into thin strips

Salt and freshly ground black pepper

NOTE:

Dividing bacon and using it in two different ways in the same recipe can add a double dose of flavor. It's a natural for sweating vegetables, where the fat perfumes the ingredients and the bacon remains fairly soft. Browned cubes are firmer and add to the texture and visual appeal.

Who would guess that a peanut-butter-and-bacon sandwich is so good it will bring tears to your eyes? It does. Add lettuce, and you have a complete meal, with every known daily nutrient needed by the average 200-pound man.

—ROGER WELSCH, *Diggin' In and Piggin' Out*

sandwiches

The Perfect BLT

The BLT—bacon, lettuce, and tomato sandwich—became popular when fresh lettuce and tomatoes became available year-round with the rapid expansion of supermarkets after World War II. According to restaurant critic John Mariani, the BLT is still the second most popular sandwich in the United States. (The simple ham sandwich is first.)

The perfect BLT is all about five simple ingredients: bread, tomatoes, lettuce, bacon, and mayonnaise. About each of these components, passionate debates occur. In the end, there is plenty of room for personal preferences and creativity, since it's all about what makes you happy, including in what order you construct it or how much of each ingredient to add. And while the classic BLT is a sandwich, look at the Deconstructed BLT Salad (page 62) and the BLT Nibbles (page 47). Here are my thoughts:

The **bread** can be an airy brioche or firm-textured country bread, like ciabatta or sourdough, slices of a fine white sandwich loaf, or even that soft, squishy one (read as Wonder Bread). Those slices should be absorbent enough to soak up every last drop of juice from the tomatoes and other ingredients as they meld together without falling apart, but not so bulky that getting your mouth around them is impossible. Part of the pleasure of a BLT comes from biting into and through all the layers at once.

While I like bread that's lightly toasted with the crust left on (it keeps things neater), other people prefer the really squishy texture of no crusts. There's wiggle room here.

However, there is less wiggle room with **tomatoes**. That's why this is really a summertime treat. Choose a tomato that is so ripe, you can smell its goodness. Mind you, it can't be overly soft, nor should it be so firm that there's no give.

When you buy tomatoes, beauty is only skin deep. Forget those perfect-looking, cottony-tasting things. Look for heirloom varieties or those grown locally (especially in your backyard) that have ripened in the sun and have been recently picked. I don't mind if they are yellow or green zebra-striped. You can even slice cherry or grape tomatoes (see BLT Nibbles on page 47). But never, ever refrigerate tomatoes before cutting.

For **lettuce**, I know purists that say iceberg lettuce is the all-American classic, but my first choice is an unblemished Bibb lettuce leaf that is washed and dried without bruising. Usually I blot it on paper towels, remove the thick rib, and set it on a clean cloth towel. I don't trim the leaf since I love when the fluttery edges hang over the bread a bit. Tender young romaine leaves are another choice; they offer a nice crunch without being tough. Lovely arugula leaves, with their peppery bite, are yet another choice. (Says Marguerite Thomas: "If you're gonna have Wonder Bread, you gotta have iceberg.")

Above all, **bacon** should be the star that carries the flavors of the other ingredients. For my money, it should be thin and crisp. Although my mom always says, "Cook my bacon until almost burned," I like mine crisp but a little flexible, so that when I bite into the sandwich it doesn't shatter into pieces. If it's thick and overcooked, it sometimes gets leathery.

I've used various specialty bacons in BLTs, from black pepper–crusted to applewood smoked. Sometimes I even use turkey bacon. Which one to use is your choice. JUST MAKE IT THE BEST YOU CAN BUY.

Finally, homemade or high-quality purchased **mayonnaise** spread over both slices of bread seals the marriage perfectly. Add, if you like, some herbs and shallots, as I do on page 62. A dash of curry paste wouldn't be bad, either. The only consideration is that it is fresh, not old tasting, to enhance one perfect sandwich.

Oh, there's one more thing I love on my BLT: sliced avocado. But that's another story.

Open-Faced Cheddar & Turkey Bacon Sandwich with Beer-Glazed Onions

A hearty open-faced sandwich where wide slices of premium turkey bacon (or regular bacon) are juxtaposed with Cheddar cheese. They are topped with robust sautéed onions deglazed with caraway-scented beer. This is a fine place for turkey bacon since it is already cooked and simply needs heating.

1. Heat the olive oil in a small skillet over medium–high heat. Add the onion and sauté until richly browned, stirring often. Stir in the beer and caraway seeds, then raise the heat and boil until the beer has almost completely evaporated. Season to taste with salt and pepper. Keep warm.

2. Turn a toaster oven on to broil. Spread the mustard on the bread. Add the bacon and cover with cheese. Broil until the cheese is melted and bubbling. Spoon the onions over the cheese and serve.

FOR EACH SANDWICH:

1½ teaspoons olive oil

1 small onion, thinly sliced

2 ounces beer

¼ teaspoon caraway seeds

Salt and freshly ground black pepper

1 slice firm country-style bread, about 4 x 4 x ½-inch thick, lightly toasted

1 teaspoon honey mustard

1 wide slice turkey bacon, cut in half crosswise

⅓ cup shredded sharp aged Cheddar cheese

Fingerprint Sandwiches

Everyone has a favorite bacon sandwich. As a child, mine was constructed of two slices of squishy, white Wonder Bread, bacon, sliced Kraft Velveeta Cheese, and a dab of mustard. Step one was spreading mustard on one slice of the soft bread and placing the cheese squarely over it. Three or four slices of bacon, hot from the fry pan, then went over the cheese. With the top slice of bread quickly clamped on, the warmth of the crisp, aromatic meat began to melt the cheese.

And as this hungry child firmly gripped the sandwich, my fingerprints were firmly imprinted on it. I could walk away for milk and return to find the well-printed sandwich unchanged from its last squeeze. It took years to convince me that toasted bread was a good idea, too.

—B.L.

Some Favorite Bacon & Cheese Sandwiches

All varieties of melted cheese are among my favorite partners for bacon. And why not? From creamy to sharp, they embrace bacon's salty-sweet taste. Serve these sandwiches open-faced or with two slices of bread. Here are some favorites:

- Provolone topped with pancetta on thin slices of lightly toasted olive or rosemary bread brushed with garlic olive oil.

- Gruyère on toasted whole-grain bread, brushed with Dijon mustard, topped with strips of crisp bacon and chopped toasted almonds.

- Cabrales (Spanish sheep's milk blue cheese) with bacon and a little quince paste on toasted raisin bread. (Other blue cheeses will also work.)

- Manchego with cranberry chutney and pepper bacon on lightly toasted thinly sliced dark bread.

- Muenster broiled with sliced tomatoes and bacon on whole-grain bread with Dijon mustard.

Provolone, Avocado & Bacon Wrap

FOR EACH SANDWICH:

1 (10-inch) flour tortilla

2–3 teaspoons mayonnaise

4 thin slices provolone or Muenster cheese

1½ teaspoons mango chutney

2 slices bacon, cooked until very crisp and blotted on paper towels

¼ ripe avocado, peeled and sliced lengthwise into 4 thin slices

Alfalfa sprouts

One of my favorite combinations. Here, I prefer whole wheat tortillas.

1. Spread the tortilla with the mayonnaise, cover with the cheese, and spread on the chutney. Lay the bacon horizontally end-to end-on the tortilla, top with avocado and sprouts, and wrap up.

Turkey, Swiss, Tomato & Bacon Wrap

FOR EACH SANDWICH:

1 (10-inch) flour tortilla

2–3 tablespoons ranch-style dressing

2 thin slices roasted turkey breast

2 thin slices Swiss cheese

1 Bibb lettuce leaf, washed and dried

2 slices bacon, cooked until very crisp and blotted on paper towels

3 very thin slices tomato

1 very thin slice red onion, separated into rings

Another easy and delicious sandwich that is heartier than the preceding one.

1. Spread the tortilla with the dressing, lay on the turkey and cheese, followed by the lettuce, bacon, and tomato. Scatter the onion over the toppings and wrap up.

A Mighty Fine Bacon Cheeseburger

6 ounces ground beef chuck

¼ teaspoon salt or to taste

Freshly ground black pepper

1½ ounces blue cheese

1 whole-grain hamburger bun, cut in half horizontally

2 slices thick-cut bacon, cooked until crisp and blotted on paper towels

1 thin slice red onion

1 Bibb lettuce leaf, washed and blotted dry

Dijon mustard mixed with high-quality mayonnaise

Pickle spears to garnish

A delicious celebration of simple good tastes! Of course, you could double or quadruple this recipe, since whoever heard of lighting a barbecue for one person? (Except our good friend and neighbor Rick Waln, who is a master griller.) Or, cook it in a cast-iron skillet. Buy ground beef with enough fat to remain juicy when it is grilled, and only mix the meat enough to blend the seasonings. I love black pepper–crusted bacon on this hamburger.

1. Spray the grill rack of a charcoal or gas grill with non-stick spray and heat until hot. Or heat a cast-iron skillet over medium–high heat until hot.

2. Mix the beef, salt, and pepper just to blend. Flatten the cheese into a 2-inch disc. Divide the hamburger meat roughly in half and flatten into 2 discs, about 3 inches in diameter. Put the cheese between the discs and pinch the edges together.

3. Cook the hamburger to medium-rare, about 3–4 minutes per side, turning once. Don't flatten the burgers with a spatula while cooking, or the juices will run out and the burger will be dry. Lay the bun, cut-side down, on the grill or in the pan and cook until lightly toasted.

4. Remove the bun, place the hamburger on top, add bacon, and serve with sliced red onions, lettuce, and grainy Dijon mustard, if desired. And don't forget a crisp pickle spear.

NOTE:

When cooking bacon in advance that you will keep warm in an oven, slightly undercook it to prevent it from becoming overly crisp and dry.

Open-Faced Eggplant & Mozzarella "Sandwiches"

In this breadless "sandwich," seen on page 78, there is a satisfying mix of textures—from creamy-smooth mozzarella to crunchy toasted bread crumbs and bacon—and a delicious marriage of tastes. Although this dish looks somewhat complicated, if you have everything ready and prepare it in the order suggested, it goes very quickly. And with what striking results! Use the best tomatoes you can find, firm and full of flavor, for a fragrant, fresh tomato sauce. Serve with slices of warm, crusty bread.

1. Cook the bacon in a heavy skillet until very crisp; remove, blot on paper towels, and reserve.

2. Meanwhile, purée the tomatoes with 1 clove of the garlic and 1 tablespoon of olive oil in a food processor until smooth. Season to taste with salt and pepper. If the tomatoes are very acidic, add a pinch of sugar and blend. Stir in the minced basil. Divide the sauce evenly among the plates, spreading it out in a large circle.

3. Combine the bread crumbs with the remaining clove of garlic and the parsley in a food processor. Process until blended. Season liberally with salt and pepper, pulse once or twice, then set aside.

4. Adjust the broiler rack close to the heat and heat the broiler. Lightly brush a baking sheet with oil. Cut the unpeeled eggplant crosswise into ¾-inch slices. Lightly brush one side of each slice with some of the remaining oil and place oiled-side up on a baking sheet. Broil until lightly browned, about 3 minutes. Turn; brush other side with oil and cook for 2 minutes more, until almost tender. Spoon about 1 teaspoon of the bread-crumb mixture onto each slice of eggplant. Continue cooking until the crumbs are toasted, about 30–45 seconds. Watch that they don't burn. Turn off the broiler.

5. Place 2 half-slices of bacon on each slice of baked eggplant and top with mozzarella; leave the pan in the turned-off oven to warm the cheese through.

6. Alternate 4 cherry or plum tomatoes halves with 4 pepper squares around the outside edge of the tomato sauce. Place a slice of eggplant in the middle of each plate. Add an unblemished basil leaf in the center with a few pieces of pepper, then sprinkle with the thinly sliced basil. Serve at once.

SERVES 6 AS AN APPETIZER

6 slices bacon or turkey bacon, cut in half crosswise

¾ pound flavorful, ripe tomatoes, peeled and seeded

2 small cloves garlic

1 tablespoon + ¼ cup extra-virgin olive oil

Salt and freshly ground black pepper

Pinch sugar, if needed

1 tablespoon minced fresh basil leaves + 6 leaves for garnish + 4 leaves cut crosswise into thin strips

¼ cup toasted whole-wheat breadcrumbs (see note)

1 tablespoon minced flat-leaf parsley

1 medium eggplant, washed

4 ounces fresh mozzarella, thinly sliced

12 tiny yellow or red cherry or grape tomatoes, split

½ roasted red or yellow pepper, cut into small squares

NOTE:

To make toasted bread crumbs, toast whole-wheat bread slices and let them cool. Tear them into chunks and pulse in a food processor to the right consistency (fine or coarse, as desired).

Have a Peanut-Butter Sandwich My Way and Hold the Jelly

Not every great sandwich builder prefers peanut butter and jelly. It's a no-brainer all right, but when it comes to incredible edibles of the hands-on style, try bacon. It's often the number-one taste and texture partner for peanut butter. When combined on toasted multigrain bread, they bring the yin and yang of sweet and salty, smooth and crunchy to the blend of aromas and tastes. Some PB&B fanciers add mayo, a move calculated to stun others.

Having been inspired by Dagwood Bumstead of comic strip fame, almost anything goes if it makes the sandwich higher. The famed Monster Burger of Hardee's and the Carnegie Deli's mile-high corned beef concoctions are worthy constructions. They are also hard to handle. Not so the PB&B, even with my favorite add-on—very thin slices of kosher garlic dill pickles—to bring moisture and tang to the party.

—B.L.

They fried the fish with bacon and were astonished; for no fish had ever seemed so delicious before. —MARK TWAIN, *The Adventures of Tom Sawyer*, Chapter 14.

seafood

Chinese Glazed Salmon

FOR THE BARBECUE SAUCE:

⅔ cup hoisin sauce

½ cup medium sherry

½ cup light brown sugar

⅓ cup soy sauce

4 cloves garlic, minced

1½ tablespoons black bean paste

1½ teaspoons Chinese five-spice
   powder

1½ teaspoons salt

Pinch red pepper flakes (optional)

These salmon fillets are a great main course when you want something special and you don't have a lot of time. They are super-easy and quick to make, as well as delicious. Serve with sautéed green beans and garlic smashed potatoes. If you want to make your own Chinese barbecue sauce, I have included a recipe below. But, there are some fine ready-made sauces, called Chinese barbecue sauce, in Asian markets and even on supermarket shelves.

MAKE THE BARBECUE SAUCE:

1. Combine all ingredients in a double boiler and simmer until the mixture begins to thicken, about 10–12 minutes. Store the unused portion in a tightly sealed jar in the refrigerator.

FOR THE FISH:

1 teaspoon oil

4 (6-ounce) salmon fillets, cut about
   1 inch wide, blotted on paper towels

Salt and freshly ground black pepper

4 tablespoons purchased or homemade Chinese barbecue sauce (see
   below)

6 slices lean bacon, cut crosswise
   in half

Thinly sliced scallions, including most
   of green parts, to garnish

BROIL THE FISH:

2. Turn on the broiler. Position the rack about 4 inches from the heat.

3. Heat the oil in a large non-stick, oven-proof skillet over medium–high heat. Add the salmon, flesh-side down, and sauté until lightly browned, about 1 minute. Turn, season the fish with salt and pepper to taste, spread the barbecue sauce over the flesh side, and drape three half-slices of bacon diagonally over the top of each fillet.

4. Transfer the fish to the broiler and cook until the bacon is crisp and the salmon is just cooked through, about 10 minutes for 1-inch-thick salmon fillets. Remove, sprinkle with scallions, and serve.

Pancetta-Wrapped Monkfish with Braised Cabbage

3 tablespoons canola oil

½ medium red cabbage, cored and finely shredded

Salt and freshly ground pepper

1 teaspoon sugar

2 teaspoons red wine vinegar or to taste

1½ pounds monkfish, about 4 medium pieces, cut in 16 1½-inch medallions; *or* 16 large sea scallops

8 thin slices pancetta or bacon, cut in half crosswise

4 wooden skewers, soaked in hot water for 15 minutes

From Sally Kofke, often my partner in bacon indulgences, comes this grilled main-course fish dish. The combination of mild, though meaty monkfish (called "poor man's lobster" until the price went sky high) served over braised cabbage is a fine marriage of tastes and textures. You can also replace the fish with scallops, if you wish.

1. Heat the oil in a medium skillet, add the cabbage, and stir to coat. When the cabbage starts to sizzle, adjust the heat to medium, add the salt and pepper to taste, and continue cooking, stirring often.

2. Once the cabbage begins to wilt, adjust the heat to low, add a little water, and cover. Cook until tender, stirring occasionally and adding a little more water as needed. Stir in the sugar and vinegar and correct the seasonings. Remove from heat and set aside, uncovered.

3. Turn the tail under on the narrow ends of the monkfish so that all pieces are the same size. Sprinkle with salt and pepper and wrap each with a piece of pancetta. Skewer with a toothpick, cutting off the ends of the pancetta if too long. (The recipe may be prepared several hours ahead to this point, then covered, refrigerated, and finished later. Remove from refrigerator 20 minutes before cooking.)

4. Pre-heat a broiler or heat a grill pan over medium–high heat. Place 4 medallions on each skewer, piercing through the fish, not the pancetta. If using a broiler or pan, cook the fish for about 5 minutes, turning 3–4 times. If using a grill, place the skewers over high heat and cook the fish for about 5 minutes, turning once. Remove them to a warm plate and tent loosely with aluminum foil.

5. While the fish is cooking, reheat the cabbage and spoon it onto a warm platter. Arrange the monkfish on top, drizzle any accumulated juices over the fish, and serve immediately.

Pancetta from Italy to America

Pancetta, also called Italian bacon, is a pork specialty that is made in every region of Italy, each with its own seasonings and style. It is made from trimmed pork bellies that are dry-cured with a combination of salt, sugar, and spices, then slightly fermented and dry-aged, but never smoked. Pancetta is sold in flat slabs or rolled, and lends its mild, slightly salty flavor to sauces, stuffing, and pasta dishes. In France, the same product is called *ventrèche*.

There are many variations in making pancetta. The spices may differ. The brining and curing times may also be different. Some products are washed with vinegars. But the result is almost always a flavor that is both sweet and salty.

Because it is cured and dehydrated, a log of pancetta will keep in your refrigerator for at least four to five months. Wrap it in plastic wrap if you will use it regularly. Otherwise, wrap it in parchment paper so it can breathe. It will continue to dry out and become harder, but the only spoilage you may have to look for is a bit of rancidity.

In America, Niman Ranch (see SUPPLIERS) makes an exceptional pancetta with a touch of cinnamon in the curing spices. Like the finest pancetta makers, they use free roaming pigs for their product. Once cured, the bellies are rolled into a cylinder and stuffed into a casing, then fermented with lactic acid for two to three days and dried and aged, like salami, for a month.

—J.P.

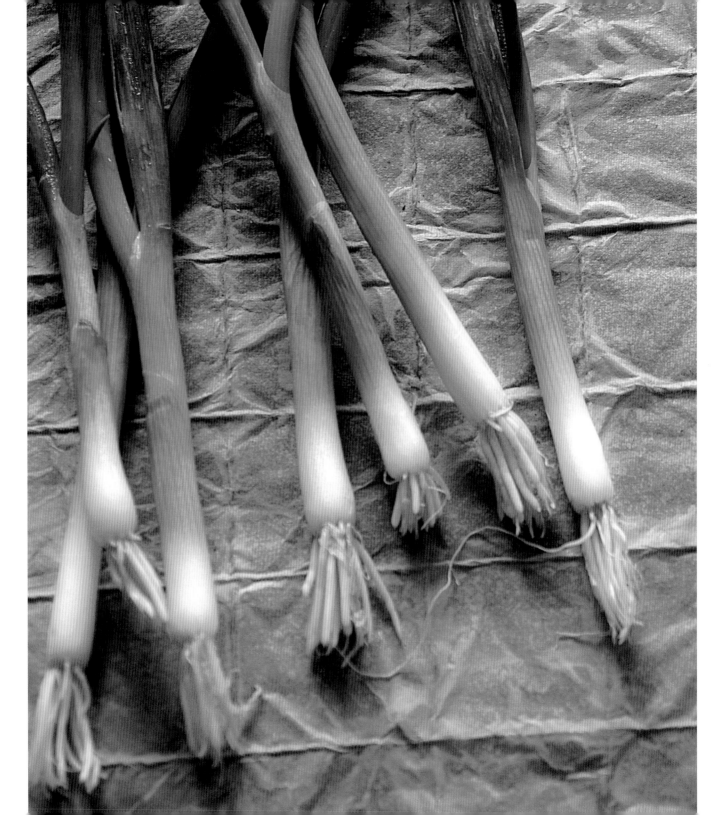

Barbecued Barramundi with Greek Yogurt Sauce

My friend Wendy Raymont suggested encasing fish fillets in bacon rind and grilling them. Although the results were superb—with the fish delicately perfumed with bacon—it takes a committed slab bacon lover (or friendly butcher) to have enough rind to do this. Instead, I buy a large slab of bacon and cut wide slices across the face of it, wrap them around the fish, and tie them into neat packages. You can remove the bacon or serve it on the fish.

Barramundi is an Australian sea bass, like Chilean sea bass, that is gaining popularity. I love the mild, sweet-tasting fish topped with Greek-style yogurt sauce, or tzatziki. Many other thick fish may be cooked this way, including halibut and grouper.

MAKE THE TZATZIKI:

1. Combine the yogurt, scallions, cucumber, garlic, and olive oil in a small bowl. Add lemon juice to taste, season to taste with salt and pepper, and chill until needed.

GRILL THE FISH:

2. Light a gas grill or charcoal barbecue and heat until medium–hot. Or, heat a broiler. Position the rack 4–5 inches from heat.

3. Lay each fillet on a piece of bacon, season with salt and pepper, add some thyme leaves, and squeeze on a little lemon juice. Turn the fish over and repeat on the second side with the salt, pepper, thyme, and lemon juice. Cover with the remaining pieces of bacon. Tie the fish together like a gift box with thick string. Grill, barbecue, or broil the fish over medium heat for 5–6 minutes, turn, and cook the second side 5 minutes more. Remove, let stand 1–2 minutes, discard the string, and serve, with or without bacon, with the yogurt sauce.

FOR THE TZATZIKI:

1 cup Greek-style unflavored whole-fat yogurt

2 scallions, including most of the green parts, trimmed and thinly sliced

1 small cucumber, finely shredded and squeezed dry in paper towels

1 large clove garlic, crushed

2 tablespoons flavorful, green extra-virgin olive oil

Lemon juice to taste

Salt and freshly ground black pepper

FOR THE FISH:

4 pieces skinless barramundi fillet, about 3 x 3½ x 1½ inches (about 6 ounces), or other bass fillets

8 pieces thinly sliced slab bacon, each about 4 x 4 inches (about 8–10 ounces total)

Salt and freshly ground black pepper

Leaves from 8 small sprigs fresh thyme

Additional lemon juice

NOTE:

Thin slices of pancetta, sold pre-sliced and in rolls, can also be wrapped around fish fillets and chicken breasts to keep them moist and add flavor while cooking. The slices will be saltier than bacon and should be removed before serving.

Grilled Trout Wrapped with Bacon

SERVES 4

4 (10–12 ounce) whole trout, cleaned
   and patted dry
Salt and freshly ground black pepper
8 sprigs fresh rosemary or sage
12 slices bacon
Lemon wedges

A camping favorite when cooked over an open fire in a fish-grilling basket. Have the trout boned, if you prefer.

1. Heat a grill or broiler until hot. Position the rack about 5–7 inches from the heat.

2. Season each trout inside and out with salt and pepper and put 2 sprigs of rosemary in the cavity. Wrap 3 bacon slices around each fish. Lay the trout in grilling racks and cook them until the skin and bacon are crisp, about 5 minutes. Turn the rack and broil 5 minutes more or until the bacon is crisp on the second side. Serve with lemon wedges.

Stir-Fried Asian Scallops with Peppers & Kale

SERVES 2

Smoky bacon adds the perfect lift to this satisfying dish of sea scallops, peppers, kale, and onions. Serve over steamed rice or Asian noodles.

1. Combine the bacon and sesame oil in a wok and cook over high heat until the bacon is separated into pieces. Add the scallops and sear on both sides, 1–2 minutes per side, turning once. Remove the scallops with a slotted spoon and set them aside.

2. Add the onion and bell pepper to the wok, stirring until wilted. Stir in the stock, soy sauce, and ginger, and bring to a boil. Stir in the coconut milk, if using. Return the scallops to the wok, then add the kale and cook until wilted over medium heat. Stir in the cilantro. Garnish with sesame seeds and serve.

3 slices thick-sliced, double-smoked bacon, finely chopped

1 tablespoon sesame oil

8 large diver or sea scallops, blotted dry

1 medium yellow onion, diced

1 yellow bell pepper with seeds and membranes removed, diced

½ cup vegetable or chicken stock

1–2 tablespoons soy sauce

1½ teaspoons ground ginger

¼ cup coconut milk (optional)

4 cups kale, coarse stems removed and cut crosswise into thin strips

¼ cup chopped cilantro

2 tablespoons black sesame seeds

 **BACON BITS**

The biggest bacon fans are 35 to 49-year-olds.

Tropical Shrimp-Pineapple/ Scallop-Mango Kabobs on the Barbie

8 (8-inch) skewers

½ cup apricot preserves

1 tablespoon soy sauce

1 (2-inch) piece fresh gingerroot

¼ teaspoon red pepper flakes

8 jumbo shrimp, peeled and deveined

8 slices thin-sliced bacon, cut crosswise
into 1-inch pieces

8 1-inch triangular pieces fresh
pineapple

8 1-inch squares red bell pepper

8 large sea scallops, small muscle
removed

8 1-inch pieces fresh mango

8 ½-inch-thick slices fresh zucchini

Salt and pepper

Grilled kabobs are a warm-weather classic. Here are two superb combi-nations: shrimp with pineapple, and scallops with mangoes. The object is to slide all the pieces on so they lay flat during cooking. When brushed with tangy apricot-ginger glaze, dinnertime couldn't be easier or more delicious.

1. Soak bamboo skewers in water for 15 minutes.

2. Combine the apricot preserves, soy sauce, gingerroot, and red pepper flakes in the jar of an electric blender and purée until smooth. Pour the glaze into a bowl and set aside.

3. Light a gas or charcoal grill and heat until hot.

4. Thread a shrimp from bottom to top through the center of the body so it lays flat on the skewer. Slide a piece of bacon onto the skewer. Add a piece of pineapple lengthwise so it lays flat, then another piece of bacon followed by a piece of bell pepper, bacon, and a scallop threaded through the sides (like a coin) so it lays flat. Again, add bacon, then a piece of mango, bacon, and a slice of zucchini so it, too, lays flat. Repeat for the remaining skewers.

6. Lightly brush the grates of the grill with oil. Lay the kabobs on the grill, sea-son them with salt and pepper, and brush generously with the apricot-ginger glaze. Close the grill and cook 3 minutes; turn, season the second side with salt and pepper, and brush with the glaze. Cook 3 minutes longer. Remove and serve over boiled rice.

Jamaican Jerked Shrimp, Mushrooms & Tomatoes

SERVES 6

These mildly spicy shrimp sautéed with bacon and tomatoes offer a concert of complex flavors. Aromatic Jamaican jerk seasoning paste (see note) and a hint of rum impart the perfect counterpoints to the sauce. Serve with quinoa or couscous, rice, or other grains to savor every last drop of goodness from the sauce.

1. Cook the bacon and oil in a heavy casserole over medium heat until about half the fat is rendered. Add the onions, mushrooms, and garlic and sauté until the onions are lightly colored, stirring often.

2. Add the shrimp and sauté over medium–high heat until they are pink on both sides, turning often. Pour in the rum, scrape up the browned cooking bits, and continue cooking over high heat for 1–2 minutes to reduce the liquid slightly, then stir in the tomatoes, jerk paste, fennel, salt, and pepper. Bring to a boil, then reduce the heat, stir in the cilantro, and simmer for 5 minutes and serve.

½ pound thick-sliced bacon, rind removed, cut into ½-inch strips

2 teaspoons oil, if bacon is very lean

1 large yellow onion, diced

4 ounces shiitake mushrooms, coarse stems removed, thickly sliced

1–2 large cloves garlic, minced

2 pounds jumbo shrimp, peeled and deveined

⅓ cup dark rum

1 28-ounce can diced tomatoes

2½–3 teaspoons Jamaican jerk paste

1 teaspoon ground fennel seed

Salt and freshly ground black pepper

¼ cup chopped cilantro

NOTE:

In Jamaica, jerk seasoning is traditional for barbecues. Along with garlic, onions, and several spices and herbs used in the mixture, the predominant ingredient is Scotch bonnet chiles. They are very hot, so go slowly when you first use jerk seasoning. You can buy it as a paste or marinade and use it to season meat, poultry, or fish. It can be brushed on before grilling or used to baste foods as they cook. Jerk seasoning is available in Caribbean groceries and many supermarkets, as well.

Drunken Mussels
Two Ways

BELGIAN STYLE WITH BACON & ALE

SERVES 2 AS
A MAIN COURSE;
4 AS AN APPETIZER

4 slices of thick-sliced meaty bacon, cut into ½-inch squares

2 teaspoons oil

1 medium onion, chopped

1 bay leaf

12 ounces Belgian ale (such as Ommegang, Chimay) or any medium-dark malty ale

2 pounds mussels, washed and debearded

2 teaspoons fresh thyme, chopped fine, for garnish (optional)

NOTE:

You can also make a version of Mussels Casino by using frozen New Zealand green-lipped mussels, which are much larger than farmed mussels and come packaged on the half-shell. Microwave them for a minute to partially thaw while they are still frozen on the half shell, then run them under the broiler with a dab of pesto and, if you like, a bit of partially pre-cooked bacon.

Our friends John and Pam Harding are bon vivants and wonderful cooks. When talking about mussels, they suggested combining the plump mollusks with either ale or white wine and bacon, in the style of Belgium or northern Italy, respectively. Either works well; both make a fine meal when served with a green salad and thick slices of crusty bread to soak up the liquid.

The Hardings look for farm-raised mussels, such as those from Prince Edward Island, because they have less grit and usually don't require debearding. Mussels are also farmed in Maine, and marketed all over the East Coast and beyond; there's a significant operation called Great Eastern Mussel Farms, based in Damariscotta. To serve the mussels in the Belgian style, include a plate of crispy French fries accompanied with mayonnaise for dunking.

1. Combine the bacon and oil in a pot large enough to accommodate the mussels, and sauté over medium heat until the bacon begins to render its fat. Stir in the onion and bay leaf and continue cooking and stirring until the bacon is brown but not burned, and the onion is soft and translucent. Add the ale, turn up the heat, and bring the liquid to a boil. Reduce the heat and simmer, covered, for 5 minutes to meld flavors.

2. Turn the heat to high, add the mussels, cover, and cook until they open, about 5 minutes. Discard any mussels that do not open. Serve in large bowls, garnished with a little chopped fresh thyme.

TICINO STYLE WITH BACON & WHITE WINE

1. Cook as above but when bacon and onions are almost cooked, add 2–3 cloves finely chopped garlic, then substitute a dry, non-oaky white wine for the beer and use parsley instead of thyme. These mussels also may be served over linguini or other thin pastas.

"A chicken in every pot" would be even better with bacon.
—ANONYMOUS

poultry & meat

110
GREEK-STYLE LAMB KABOBS WITH
PEPPERS, ONIONS & TOMATOES

112
BEEF & VEGETABLE POT PIE IN PEPPER-BACON CRUST

114
OLD-FASHIONED SHEPHERD'S PIE

116
DEVILISH SHORT RIBS

119
BELGIAN RABBIT IN CHERRY BEER

120
CRISPY OVEN-ROASTED CHICKEN WITH SAGE & BACON

122
BASQUE CHICKEN IN RED WINE

123
CORNISH GAME HENS WITH CIDER-GLAZED CABBAGE &
SAUTÉED APPLES

124
ROAST SQUABS STUFFED WITH
PORCINI & CHESTNUTS

127
SPICY TURKEY MEATLOAF

128
SAUERKRAUT, KIELBASA & BACON

Greek-Style Lamb Kabobs with Peppers, Onions & Tomatoes

SERVES 4

¼ cup fragrant olive oil

2 tablespoons fresh lemon juice

4 cloves garlic, minced

1 teaspoon fresh oregano leaves *or* ¼ teaspoon dried leaves

1 teaspoon fresh thyme leaves *or* ¼ teaspoon dried leaves

1½ pounds lamb cut from the leg into 1½-inch cubes (about 20 cubes)

Salt and freshly ground black pepper

4 12-inch wooden skewers soaked for 15 minutes in water.

4 slices thick-sliced bacon, cut crosswise into 1-inch pieces

8 large cherry tomatoes

8 1½-inch pearl onions or cippolini onions, peeled, with an "X" cut in each root end and blanched

1 large red or green bell pepper with seeds and membranes removed, cut into 1-inch squares

Sprigs of fresh thyme to garnish (optional)

Greek olives to garnish (optional)

Tzatziki (page 99)

I love food that is barbecued or cooked on a gas grill. For these Greek-inspired kabobs, squares of bacon threaded between the meat and vegetables make them even tastier. Serve over tossed mixed greens or cooked rice with the Greek yogurt sauce, tzatziki, on page 99. Pita bread cut into wedges is a nice addition.

Once the lamb is marinated, the kabobs may be threaded onto long metal or 12-inch wooden skewers several hours ahead of time and refrigerated. If you use wooden skewers, remember to first soak them in water for at least 15 minutes.

1. Combine the olive oil, lemon juice, garlic, oregano, and thyme together in a large resealable plastic bag. Add the lamb cubes, season with salt and pepper, seal the bag, and marinate for at least 1 hour or overnight in the refrigerator, turning a couple of times.

2. Heat a barbecue or gas grill to high. Remove the meat from the marinade. For each 12-inch skewer, start by threading a tomato onto the skewer. Add a piece of bacon doubled over, a cube of lamb, a piece of bacon doubled over, and an onion. Continue with lamb, pepper, lamb, tomato, lamb, and onion, and finally lamb and pepper, putting a piece of bacon on either side of each cube of lamb in the sequence. Repeat with remaing skewers.

3. Lightly oil the grill. Place the skewers on the grill, cover, and cook until the meat is medium-rare, about 1–2 minutes per side, turning until all four sides are cooked, about 8 minutes total cooking time. To serve, transfer the skewers to plates with salad or cooked rice on them. Garnish with the thyme sprigs and Greek olives; spoon on the tzatziki, and serve.

FOR THE CRUST:

4 slices bacon, cooked until very crisp
and blotted on paper towels

1¼ cups flour

½ teaspoon salt

8 tablespoons (1 stick) cold unsalted
butter, cut into pieces

2–4 tablespoons cold water

¾ teaspoon very coarsely ground
black peppercorns

FOR THE FILLING:

2 each medium carrots, parsnips, and
turnips, peeled and cut into 1- x ½- x
½-inch pieces (about ¾ cup each)

20 pearl onions, an "X" cut in each
root end

3 tablespoons unsalted butter, chilled

1¼ pounds well-trimmed filet mignon,
cut into 1-inch cubes, blotted dry

2 ounces slab bacon with rind
removed, cut in ¼-inch cubes

4 large shallots, thinly sliced

½ cup full-bodied red wine

¼ cup Cognac or brandy

½ cup veal demi-glace (see page 55)

¼ cup finely chopped flat-leaf parsley
+ 1 tablespoon for garnish

2 tablespoons flour

Salt and freshly ground black pepper

Beef & Vegetable Pot Pie in Pepper-Bacon Crust

These sophisticated, open-faced personal-size pot pies have flaky crusts spiked with tiny bits of bacon and coarsely ground pepper. The filling is a mouth-watering combination of seared filet mignon, roasted root vegetables, and a full-bodied red wine–Cognac reduction.

MAKE THE CRUST:

1. Combine the cooked bacon, flour, and salt in a food processor and process until the bacon is finely chopped. Add the butter and pulse until the mixture resembles fine meal. Pour in 2 tablespoons of water and process just until the mixture comes together into a ball, adding additional teaspoons of water if the pastry is too dry. Add the pepper and pulse to mix. Remove the pastry, divide it into 4 equal pieces, dust lightly with flour, and flatten into a small disc. Cover with plastic wrap and refrigerate for 30 minutes.

2. Preheat your oven to 400°F.

3. On a lightly floured board, roll the pastry discs into 8-inch circles about ⅛ inch thick. Transfer to individual 6-inch pie pans. Trim the excess pastry and decorate the edges with the tines of a fork. Prick each crust several times. Lay a piece of aluminum foil on each crust, smoothing it against the edges, and weight it with dried beans or rice. Bake in the middle of the oven just until the crusts are set, 6–8 minutes. Remove the foil and beans, return the crusts to the oven, and bake until golden brown, 12–14 minutes. Turn the oven down to 200°F. Keep the crusts warm until the final assembly, or let them cool and reheat when needed.

MEANWHILE, PREPARE THE FILLING:

4. Blanch the carrots, parsnips, turnips, and pearl onions in boiling salted water until just cooked through but still firm, about 2–4 minutes. Remove the pieces with a slotted spoon as they become tender; shock them in cold water, drain, and blot dry. Heat 1 tablespoon of butter in a large skillet until hot. Add the vegetables and sauté until lightly browned, 2–3 minutes, shaking the pan occasionally. Keep warm.

5. Heat another tablespoon of butter in another large skillet over high heat. Quickly sear the meat on all sides, 2–3 minutes for medium-rare, then transfer it to the pan with the vegetables.

6. Adjust the heat to medium, stir the bacon cubes into the skillet, and cook for 2 minutes, turning often. Stir in the shallots and cook over medium–high heat until they are light brown, 2 minutes. Pour in the wine, Cognac, and demi-glace and boil for 1 minute to reduce the liquid, scraping up any browned cooking bits. Stir in the parsley and keep the sauce warm on low heat.

7. If the sauce is too thin, blend the remaining tablespoon of butter and flour together with your fingers; whisk it by bits into the sauce until it thickens. Do not let it boil. Return the meat and any juices that have accumulated along with the vegetables to the pan, turning to coat evenly. Season to taste with salt and pepper. Divide the meat, vegetables, and sauce evenly among the warm piecrusts and serve with a little parsley sprinkled on top. Or tent with foil (do not seal) and keep in a warm oven for up to an hour.

Old-Fashioned Shepherd's Pie

SERVES 4 GENEROUSLY

1½ pounds baking potatoes, peeled and coarsely chopped

4 ounces double-smoked slab bacon with the rind removed, cut into 1- x ½- x ½-inch pieces

1 large yellow onion, finely chopped

1 red bell pepper with seeds and membranes removed, finely chopped

2 cloves garlic, minced

1 pound lean ground lamb or beef, or a combination of both

1 (14½-ounce) can diced tomatoes

1 cup beef stock

⅓ cup chopped flat-leaf parsley

1 tablespoon Worcestershire sauce

½ teaspoon dried thyme leaves

Salt and freshly ground black pepper

2 tablespoons cornstarch

1 (10-ounce) package frozen petite peas, defrosted and blotted dry

2 tablespoons unsalted butter

4–6 tablespoons milk

Shepherd's pie is as homey as meatloaf but more glamorous and a one-dish meal, as well. Ground lamb (or beef), with a hint of smoky bacon, marries so well with layers of peas and mashed potatoes, it'll take you back to your childhood. You can make it ahead and reheat it, if you prefer.

This dish was so-named because it was commonplace food for sheepherders who ate in the morning or at noon before tending their flocks.

1. In a saucepan, cover the potatoes with water, add a little salt, and bring to a boil; cook until the potatoes are tender when a sharp knife is inserted into the center, then drain.

2. Meanwhile, put the bacon in a heavy pot and sauté it over medium heat until the pieces are lightly browned on all sides but still moist in the center and fat covers the bottom of the pan. Remove the bacon, blot on paper towels, and set aside. Discard all but 3 tablespoons of the fat.

3. Stir in the onion, bell pepper, and garlic, and cook over medium–high heat until the onion is wilted and starts to color, 3 minutes. Add the lamb or beef, tomatoes, reserved bacon, stock, parsley, Worcestershire sauce, thyme, and salt and pepper. Add a little water if the liquid does not cover the meat. Adjust the heat down, cover, and simmer for 20–25 minutes. Taste to adjust the seasonings.

4. Stir ¼ cup of the cooking liquid and the cornstarch together in a small dish until smooth; stir the mixture into the meat, blending well. Bring to a boil to thicken, then turn off the heat. Scrape the meat mixture into a medium-sized gratin dish, or a large, deep pie plate. Spoon the peas over the mixture and leave undisturbed for a few minutes so the top sets slightly.

5. Preheat your oven to 400°F.

6. Pass the potatoes through a food mill or potato ricer. Stir in the butter and enough milk to make the potatoes creamy and fluffy. Season to taste with salt and pepper. Carefully spoon the potatoes evenly on top of the casserole, trying not to disturb the surface of the meat filling. Using a metal spatula, spread the potatoes out over the filling in a smooth layer, then decorate with the tines of a fork. Or, using a pastry bag fitted with a decorative tip, pipe the mashed potatoes over the meat filling.

7. Transfer the dish to the oven and bake until the mixture begins to bubble up around the edges of the potatoes and the potatoes are golden brown, about 20 minutes. If the top is not browned, run the pie under the broiler for a few minutes to color. Watch that it doesn't burn. Remove and let stand 5–10 minutes before serving.

 **BACON BITS**

My favorite animal is bacon. —**Fran Lebowitz**

Devilish Short Ribs

6 ounces double-smoked slab bacon with rind removed, cut into ½-inch cubes

6 large, meaty beef short ribs, patted dry

2 medium carrots, peeled and coarsely chopped

1 large yellow onion, coarsely chopped

6 cups beef stock

1½ cups full-bodied red wine

2 large red bell peppers, roasted, peeled and seeded

2 dried ancho chiles

1 jalapeño pepper, split and seeded

6 cloves garlic, bruised

5 bay leaves

½ cup chopped flat-leaf parsley

1 tablespoon black peppercorns

½–¾ teaspoon smoked hot or semi-sweet paprika, preferably Spanish, according to taste

Salt and freshly ground black pepper

Chopped cilantro, to garnish (optional)

These lusty but oh-so-tender short ribs simply fall off the bone. The ancho chile–laced braising liquid is reduced and combined with bell peppers and a touch of smoked Spanish paprika or Pimentón de la Vera. It really boosts the flavors. Serve over hominy grits or polenta. A recipe from Brandon Scimeca, former executive chef at Interlaken Inn, in Lakeville, Connecticut, inspired this dish, shown on page 108.

1. Preheat your oven to 350°F.

2. Put the bacon in a large, heavy casserole and cook over medium–high until the pieces are lightly browned and have rendered most of their fat but are still moist in the center. Remove, blot on paper towels, and set aside. Reserve 2 tablespoons of fat in the pan. Add the short ribs and lightly brown on all sides. Do this in batches, if necessary, so you brown rather than steam the meat. Remove to a bowl.

3. Add the carrots and onions, and sauté them until soft and lightly browned. Add the stock and bring to a boil, stirring up all the browned cooking bits. Pour in the wine; add the bell peppers, ancho chiles, jalapeño, garlic, bay leaves, parsley, and peppercorns along with reserved short ribs and bacon. Cover the pot and transfer it to the oven to braise for 3 hours, stirring occasionally.

4. Remove the pot from the oven. Using a slotted spoon, lift out the bell peppers and reserve. Remove the short ribs to a large platter, tent with aluminum foil, and set aside. Skim off as much fat as possible, then strain the braising liquid into a clean pot and, over high heat, reduce it by half. Stir in the paprika and season to taste with salt and pepper.

5. In a food processor, purée the bell peppers with the reduced braising liquid until smooth. If desired, pour the purée through a fine strainer. Reheat if necessary. Serve the short ribs with a generous amount of sauce ladled over them and a little cilantro to garnish, if desired.

Bacon Brings More than Sizzle

During World War II, Americans saved tin foil, string, and bacon fat to help in the war effort. I thought the latter was a curious thing to set aside in coffee cans and periodically carry to the meat market. In exchange for the bacon and lard drippings, the butcher gave my parents a set amount of ration coupons that could be applied toward the purchase of meat or sugar.

As a child, I didn't know what became of the bacon fat. Ruth Ross, an aunt, added lye to it to make a harsh soap for rugged cleaning. But soap was not the primary purpose for the nationwide collection of animal fats.

Making explosives to fight the war was its assignment.

A chemical reaction called "saponification" results from mixing animal fat or vegetable oil with a strong alkali. It produces glycerin, which was used in making dynamite, nitroglycerin, and blast gelatin as well as the smokeless powders Cordite and Ballistite.

A man whose experience went from pig to POW! was Al Seiler. Formerly a chemical engineer at an Akron, Ohio, tire plant, he had become the butcher partner in a grocery store (today that store is the Midwest's legendary West Point Market). Mr. Seiler recalls doling out ration stamps good for butter and meat in exchange for drippings collected from cooking meat he'd first sold the customers. Trucks from the Portage Rendering Company made regular rounds to pick up the fats from grocery stores and markets in the area. They were paid 12 to 15 cents a pound. At an explosives manufacturing facility, the extracted glycerin was blended with nitric acid to make nitroglycerin.

Animal fats were the principal source of glycerin until the late 1940s.   —B.L.

Belgian Rabbit in Cherry Beer

SERVES 4-6

This fork-tender rabbit stew was inspired by the food I tasted in Belgium, where hundreds of local beers are used instead of wine for braising meats and poultry. This rabbit is simmered in kriek lambic, *or cherry beer, along with mushrooms, pearl onions, and dried cherries. It's a real feast. A touch of tangy crème fraîche is stirred in just before serving. Serve with couscous, polenta, or small roasted Yukon gold potatoes.*

1. Heat a large, heavy casserole or Dutch oven over medium–high heat, add the bacon, and sauté until the pieces are lightly browned on all sides and have rendered most of their fat but are still moist inside, about 6 minutes. Remove with a slotted spoon and blot on paper towels. Set aside. Reserve the fat in the pan.

2. Lightly dredge the rabbit pieces in flour, patting them to remove excess flour. Add 1 tablespoon of the oil to the casserole and heat over medium–high heat until hot. Add the rabbit pieces and cook until richly browned on both sides, about 3–4 minutes per side, turning once. Cook only as many pieces as will fit comfortably in the bottom of the pan without crowding, adding additional oil as needed until all the pieces are cooked. Remove the pieces to a bowl with a slotted spoon, season generously with salt and pepper, and set aside.

3. Add another tablespoon of oil, stir in the carrot, celery, and onion, and sauté until lightly colored, 6–7 minutes; add the garlic and cook 30 seconds longer. Pour in the cherry beer and stock and bring the liquid to a boil over high heat, scraping up all the browned bits. Cook for 1 minute.

4. Return the rabbit and bacon to the casserole; add the parsley, thyme, and bay leaf; cover and simmer over medium–low heat for 45 minutes.

5. While the rabbit is simmering, heat the remaining tablespoon of oil in a large, heavy skillet over medium–high heat. Add the pearl onions and sauté them until lightly browned on all sides, about 6–8 minutes, shaking the pan to cook them evenly. After the rabbit has simmered for 45 minutes, uncover the pot and stir in the onions, mushrooms, and cherries; boil gently for 5–10 minutes to thicken the sauce. Remove the bay leaf, stir in the crème fraîche, and taste to adjust seasonings. Serve the rabbit garnished with a little parsley.

4 ounces slab bacon with rind removed, cut into 1- x ½- x ½-inch pieces

Flour for dredging

1 (2½- to 3-pound) rabbit, dressed, cut into serving pieces, blotted dry

3–4 tablespoons oil

Salt and freshly ground black pepper

1 medium carrot, peeled and finely chopped

1 medium rib celery, finely chopped

1 medium onion, finely chopped

1 large clove garlic, minced

1 (12-ounce) bottle Belgian cherry beer

½ cup chicken stock

¼ cup finely chopped flat-leaf parsley + additional parsley to garnish

2 large sprigs fresh thyme

1 large bay leaf

16–18 pearl onions, with an "X" cut in each root end, or frozen pearl onions

8 ounces small white mushrooms, wiped, trimmed, and quartered

½ cup dried cherries

2 ounces crème fraîche or sour cream

Crispy Oven-Roasted Chicken with Sage & Bacon

SERVES 4

1 (3–3¼-pound) whole chicken with extra fat removed, rinsed under cold water and blotted dry

6–8 fresh sage leaves + small sage leaves to garnish

Salt and freshly ground pepper

½ lemon

8 slices bacon

2 tablespoon olive or vegetable oil

2 carrots, peeled and coarsely chopped

2 stalks celery, coarsely chopped

1 large onion, coarsely chopped

¾ cup white wine

¾ cup chicken stock

2 tablespoons chopped flat-leaf parsley

A couple of tricks help this beautiful roast chicken to become fragrant, juicy, and perfectly crisp. Sage leaves are tucked under the skin before cooking to perfume the meat and add a decorative touch. The chicken is left uncovered overnight in the refrigerator to help seal in moisture, and strips of bacon are laced over the breast during the first half of cooking to automatically baste the bird. With all of that help, this chicken can't help but be delicious. The simple pan gravy is made from the roasted vegetables on which the chicken cooks, along with a little added stock and wine. Green Pea & Pancetta Packets (page 152) are a nice accompaniment.

1. Starting at the neck, loosen the skin from the breast and drumsticks by gently pushing your fingers between the skin and the meat. Slide the sage leaves under the skin and arrange decoratively. Season the cavity with salt and pepper, and squeeze in the lemon juice. Put the squeezed lemon half inside the cavity. Place the chicken on a cake rack over a plate and leave it uncovered in refrigerator overnight, or for at least 8 hours.

2. Preheat your oven to 450°F.

3. Lay the strips of bacon crisscrossing diagonally on the chicken breast to cover it. Add 1 tablespoon olive oil to a heavy gratin or shallow roasting pan just large enough to hold the chicken. Add the carrots, celery, and onion. Brush the remaining oil over the chicken legs, and put the chicken on top of the vegetables. Put the pan in the oven with the legs of the bird facing toward the back of the oven.

4. Adjust the heat down to 400°F, and roast until the bacon is crisp, about 30–40 minutes, basting the legs with the pan drippings once or twice during this time. Remove the bacon and reserve to serve, if desired, with the chicken. Baste the chicken, and return it to the oven.

5. After the chicken has cooked for 1 hour, pour the wine and stock over the vegetables, stirring up all the browned cooking bits, and continue roasting until the skin is a rich brown and the legs move easily in their sockets, about another 40–50 minutes, basting every 20 minutes with pan drippings. Remove the chicken from the oven.

6. Turn the oven off. Transfer the chicken to a platter and keep warm in the oven while finishing the sauce. Scrape the vegetables and pan drippings into the jar of an electric blender and purée until almost smooth. Season to taste with salt and pepper, then stir in the parsley.

7. Cut the chicken into serving pieces and put on plates or a platter. Ladle a small amount of sauce over the pieces of chicken, add a sage leaf, and serve. Pass the remaining sauce at the table.

Basque Chicken in Red Wine

SERVES 6

Cooking spray

6 large (6-ounce) skinless chicken thighs, patted dry

Salt and freshly ground black pepper

½ pound lean, thick-cut bacon, cut crosswise into ½-inch strips

2 large onions, coarsely chopped

1 large green bell pepper with seeds and membranes removed, coarsely chopped

1 large red bell pepper with seeds and membranes removed, coarsely chopped

5–6 sage leaves, julienned or 1 tablespoon dried sage leaf, crumbled

2 teaspoons fresh chopped thyme or 1 teaspoon dry thyme leaves

1¼ cups hearty red wine

¾ cup pitted kalamata or other imported black olives

½ cup sour cream (optional)

I first tasted chicken simmered in red wine years ago in the Basque region of southern France. Until then, I thought cooking chicken in white wine was the thing to do. Today we think of using red wine with poultry and even fish where the dish's other ingredients have strong flavors. Colorful peppers and olives give this simple dish a hearty taste. It can be made a day or two ahead of time and slowly reheated. Breasts or a whole 3½-pound chicken may be substituted.

1. Spray a large, heavy casserole with cooking spray and heat over high heat. Add the chicken, meaty sides down, and cook until lightly browned, 2–3 minutes. Turn and cook the second side until lightly browned. Remove the chicken to a bowl and season with salt and pepper. Discard any fat in the pan.

2. Add the bacon to the pan and cook over medium–high heat until the pieces begin to separate and fat covers bottom of pan, about 3–4 minutes. Add the onions and peppers and cook until onions are wilted and lightly colored, 6–7 minutes. Stir in the sage and thyme. Pour in the red wine, adjust the heat to high, and boil for 5–6 minutes to reduce slightly, stirring up all the browned cooking bits.

3. Return the chicken along with the olives to the pot, reduce the heat so the liquid is just simmering, cover, and cook for another 15–20 minutes, stirring occasionally, or until the chicken is cooked through. Stir in the sour cream, if using, taste to adjust seasonings, and serve.

Cornish Game Hens with Cider-Glazed Cabbage & Sautéed Apples

SERVES 4

In France, braised cabbage is a classic partner for partridge. Rather than waiting for a game bird, I use Cornish game hens. When the pairing is enhanced with cider, bacon, and tangy Granny Smith apples, I find it irresistible. The browned birds, steamed over the cabbage, are very juicy and tender; they are topped with sautéed apples. Serve them with spaetzle or mashed potatoes.

1. Put the bacon in a large, deep skillet or casserole and slowly render the fat over medium heat but do not brown the cubes, about 6–8 minutes. Remove the bacon with a slotted spoon and drain on paper towels. Leave 1 tablespoon of fat in pan; reserve the remaining fat.

2. Heat the bacon fat in the pan over medium–high heat, add the game hens, flesh-side down, and cook until golden brown, about 5–6 minutes; turn and cook the second side until browned. Transfer to a bowl, season generously with salt and pepper, and set aside. Wipe out the pan.

3. Add another tablespoon of fat to the pot. When hot, add the cabbage and sauté over medium–high heat until it starts to wilt and cook down, turning often. Pour in the cider and enough stock to come halfway up the cabbage, bring the liquid to a boil, and cook for 2 minutes.

4. Stir in the reserved bacon and lay the game hens, flesh-side up, on top. Lower the heat so the liquid just simmers, cover the pan, and cook gently for 20 minutes. Turn off the heat and leave covered for 10 minutes more.

5. Meanwhile, heat the butter in a large skillet over medium–high heat. Add the apples and sauté them until they begin to brown. Sprinkle them with the sugar, turning to coat evenly, and continue cooking over low heat until lightly caramelized. Squeeze on the lemon juice, turn again, and keep warm.

6. Serve the game hens over cabbage. Spoon the sautéed apples over game hens, drizzle with the pan juices, and garnish with a little parsley.

½ pound slab bacon with rind removed, cut into ½-inch cubes

2 Cornish game hens, cut in half lengthwise, backbones and wingtips removed, blotted on paper towels

Salt and freshly ground black pepper

1½ pounds green cabbage, cored, quartered, and shredded (about 8 cups)

¾ cup apple cider

1–1½ cups chicken stock

2 tablespoons unsalted butter

2–3 large Granny Smith apples, peeled, cored, and cut into eighths

2 tablespoons sugar

Few drops fresh lemon juice

Chopped flat-leaf parsley, to garnish

NOTE:

Laying sliced bacon on the breast of a bird while it cooks—or ***barding*** it— automatically bastes it and helps keep it moist. If the bird isn't browned first, remove the bacon before the end of the cooking time so the skin gets crisp and golden.

Roast Squabs Stuffed with Porcini & Chestnuts

1 lemon

8 (1-pound) squabs, rinsed inside and out with cool water and blotted dry, excess fat removed

Freshly ground black pepper

2 ounces dried porcini mushrooms

4 tablespoons olive oil

1 (6-ounce) sweet Italian sausage, casing removed

1 large yellow onion, chopped

2 medium-sized stalks of celery, trimmed and chopped

24 chestnuts, freshly roasted *or* 1 (15½-ounce) can or jar unsweetened chestnuts, drained and chopped

½ cup currants

⅓ cup Marsala

3 tablespoons finely chopped flat-leaf parsley

1 teaspoon salt or to taste

¼ cup toasted bread crumbs

2 sprigs fresh rosemary *or* 2 tablespoons dried rosemary (see note)

8 slices pancetta or bacon

1½ cups dry vermouth

1 tablespoon unsalted butter, at room temperature (optional)

1 tablespoon flour (optional)

48 seedless red grapes, stems removed, washed

This dish reminds me of autumn in Tuscany when porcini mushrooms and squabs are both in season. Squabs, or pigeons, have a special flavor— some say slightly reminiscent of liver—that is complemented by well-seasoned stuffing. Wrapping or barding lean birds with bacon while they roast (see note on page 123) keeps them moist and succulent. Here, porcini and chestnuts are combined with sausages, currants, and Marsala. The sauce is made with the pan juices and red grapes.

1. Squeeze the lemon juice into the cavity of each squab. Season the birds liberally with black pepper.

2. Soak the porcini mushrooms in warm water until soft, 25–30 minutes. Rinse to remove all grit and cut off any fibrous pieces, then coarsely chop the mushrooms. Reserve. Strain the liquid through several layers of cheesecloth, a coffee filter, or a fine strainer lined with paper towels into a saucepan. Bring this liquid to a boil, cook until reduced to ½ cup, then set aside.

3. In a large, heavy skillet, heat 1 tablespoon of olive oil over medium–high heat until hot and fragrant. Add the sausage, chopping it into small pieces with a wooden spatula or spoon, and cook until no longer pink, 4–5 minutes. Stir in the onion and celery, cook until translucent, then add the porcini, chestnuts, currants, Marsala, parsley, and salt and pepper; stir to blend well. Raise the heat to high and boil until the liquid almost completely evaporates, about 2–3 minutes. Add the bread crumbs and mix well.

4. Divide the stuffing evenly among the squabs. Stuff the birds, then tuck the wingtips under and tie the legs together. In a large, heavy casserole, heat the remaining oil until fragrant. Brown a few birds at a time, making sure to keep the oil hot. Turn them to brown all sides, then remove and set aside.

5. Lay 3–4 rosemary leaves on each bird and wrap them with the pancetta.
   Return the birds, breast-side up, to the casserole. Adjust the heat to medium,
   cover the pot, and cook gently for 35–40 minutes, basting twice during this
   time. The squabs are done when the thigh moves easily in the socket and the
   juices run clear when the thigh is pricked.

6. Transfer the squabs to a heated oven-proof platter. Discard the bacon. If the
   birds are not nicely browned, run them briefly under the broiler. Skim as
   much fat as possible from the casserole. Deglaze the pan with vermouth,
   scraping up the browned cooking bits; boil until almost completely evaporated.
   Add the reduced mushroom liquid and return to a boil. For a thicker sauce,
   blend the softened butter and flour together in a small bowl with your fingers,
   and whisk it into the hot liquid in small pieces. Immediately turn off the heat.
   Season with salt and pepper to taste. Stir in the grapes and heat through.
   Serve the birds on heated plates with a generous spoonful of sauce.

NOTE:
To refresh dried rosemary leaves, put
them in a small bowl and cover with
hot water for about 2 minutes, then
drain and blot dry.

Spicy Turkey Meatloaf

This somewhat spicy turkey meatloaf, perfumed with exotic Indian seasonings, sweet Thai chili sauce, and topped with thinly sliced Gypsy bacon (see Baconology on page 9), has plenty of taste and is deliciously juicy. You can easily make this in a food processor, but only pulse briefly to blend the ingredients so the mixture stays light. Serve it warm, accompanied by raita—*a mixture of yogurt, diced cucumbers, mint, and roasted cumin seeds—and mango chutney. Or use the Greek tzatziki sauce on page 99. When cooled, the meatloaf also makes a great sandwich (see note below).*

1. Preheat your oven to 350°F.

2. Heat the olive oil in a large skillet over medium–high heat. Add the onions and sauté until they are wilted and lightly browned, about 5–6 minutes. Stir in the curry, cumin, and cayenne. Set aside.

3. Combine the cooked bacon, garlic, carrot, red bell pepper, and cilantro in a food processor and pulse until finely chopped. Add the bread crumbs and 3 tablespoons of the Thai chili sauce, salt, and pepper and pulse until blended.

4. Add the turkey, eggs, and reserved onions and pulse until just blended. Do not over-mix. Transfer the mixture to a 9" x 5" x 3" loaf pan, patting lightly until smooth. Spread the remaining chili sauce over the top. Cover with the bacon and cook for about 1 hour 10 minutes, or until the juices run clear. Remove from oven and let stand 5 to 10 minutes, pour off any juices from the pan, then slice and serve, or let the meatloaf cool and serve at room temperature.

3 tablespoons olive oil

2 cups finely chopped onions

1 tablespoon curry powder

2 teaspoons ground cumin

½ teaspoon cayenne pepper

6 strips bacon, cooked until crisp, blotted on paper towels and crumbled

2 large cloves garlic

2 medium carrots, peeled and coarsely chopped

1 red bell pepper with seeds and membranes removed, coarsely chopped

½ cup chopped cilantro

1 cup fresh bread crumbs

½ cup sweet Thai chili sauce

1 teaspoon salt or to taste

Freshly ground black pepper

2 pounds ground turkey

2 eggs, lightly beaten

2 slices Gypsy bacon or 3 slices thick-sliced bacon

IDEA:

For a sandwich, cut the meatloaf crosswise into about a ½-inch-thick slice. Serve open-face atop lightly toasted Italian country bread with a romaine lettuce leaf, a slice of sweet Vidalia onion, and generous spoonful of tzatziki.

Sauerkraut, Kielbasa & Bacon

SERVES 4-6

3 tablespoons unsalted butter

2 large onions, chopped

2 large cloves garlic, minced

2 pounds sauerkraut, rinsed and
squeezed dry

1 pound baking potatoes, peeled and
coarsely shredded

2 Granny Smith apples, peeled, if
desired, and coarsely shredded

1 cup dry white wine

1 cup chicken stock

4 tablespoons coarse-grained
Pommery-style mustard

3 large bay leaves

1 teaspoon caraway seeds

1 teaspoon canola oil

1 pound turkey or pork kielbasa or
chicken sausages, cut into chunks

4 ounces sliced turkey bacon, cut into
¾-inch pieces

Salt and coarsely ground black pepper

4 tablespoons chopped flat-leaf parsley

Inspired by a traditional Alsatian or Polish partnership of sausages and sauerkraut, this updated version uses turkey bacon and turkey kielbasa or chicken sausages along with shredded potatoes and apples. Naturally, the dish is equally satisfying when made with traditional bacon and kielbasa. Serve it with coarse-grained mustard and thick slices of rustic dark bread.

Because turkey bacon is so lean, the onion is browned in butter and the bacon is added toward the end of the cooking to retain the maximum flavor. If using conventional bacon, sauté the onions and bacon together until the onions are golden brown. You won't need the butter.

1. Melt the butter in a large, heavy pot over medium–high heat. Add the onions and sauté them until golden brown, stirring occasionally. Add the garlic, cook 30 seconds; stir in the sauerkraut, potatoes, and apples, and cook for 1 minute.

2. Pour in the wine and stock, add the mustard, bay leaves, and caraway seeds, and bring to a boil; reduce the heat, cover, and simmer until the potatoes are tender, about 35–40 minutes, stirring occasionally. While the sauerkraut cooks, heat the oil in a large skillet over medium–high heat. Add the kielbasa or sausage chunks and brown them on all sides.

3. Remove the cover from the sauerkraut, stir in the turkey bacon and sausages, and season to taste with salt and pepper. Deglaze the skillet with a little wine and pour the liquid into the pot; continue cooking for 30 minutes longer or until the mixture is a rich brown, stirring occasionally. Before serving, remove the bay leaves, stir in the parsley, and cook for 1 minute longer.

NOTE:

With bacon and potatoes being such a fine combination, a food processor with a shredding disc is invaluable. The machine saves a lot of time and labor.

Better beans and bacon in peace than cakes and ale in fear.

—**AESOP**, Greek fabulist *(620–560 B.C.)*

pasta, beans & grains

132
VENETIAN-STYLE SAVORY TORTA

135
GNOCCHI WITH CHICKEN LIVERS,
PEAS & LARDONS

136
SPAGHETTI CARBONARA

137
NICOLE'S CARBONARA

138
DON VITTORIO'S RIGATONI WITH
TOMATO-VODKA SAUCE

140
MACATTACARONI

143
RISOTTO WITH SHRIMP,
ASPARAGUS & PANCETTA

144
BLAZIN' BAKED BEANS

145
MOROS Y CRISTIANOS
(BLACK BEANS & RICE)

Venetian-Style Savory Torta

In Italian the word "pasta" is any kind of dough used for pastry and cakes, macaroni, or all pasta. Sally and Gene Kofke and I were served this superb 18th century–style pasta torta—filled with mixed bitter greens, mushrooms, and pancetta—while visiting our friends Vittor-Luigi and Wilma Braga Rosa, who live in Italy's Veneto region. Thanks to Wilma for sharing this recipe for a satisfying first course or even hearty lunch dish. Choose the greens available to you. She used a mixture of spinach, Swiss chard, and radicchio. It is delicious either warm or at room temperature.

FOR THE CRUST:

2 cups unbleached flour

¼ teaspoon salt

6 tablespoons cold unsalted butter, cut in small pieces

2 egg yolks

3 tablespoons extra-virgin olive oil

6–8 tablespoons cold water

FOR THE FILLING:

¾ pound pancetta or ventrèche, cut in ¼-inch pieces

1 small yellow onion, chopped

½ pound shiitake or other wild mushrooms, stems removed, wiped, and coarsely chopped

1 pound Swiss chard, trimmed and washed, leaves cut from stems

½ pound kale, ribs discarded and leaves washed

Additional olive oil, as needed

Salt and freshly ground pepper

4 ounces Asiago cheese, thinly sliced

2 large eggs + 1 egg yolk

⅓ cup lightly toasted pine nuts

MAKE THE CRUST:

1. Combine the flour and salt in a food processor and pulse to mix. Add the butter and pulse until the mixture resembles coarse meal. Whisk together the egg yolks, olive oil, and 5 tablespoons cold water and drizzle in a circle over the flour. Process briefly until the mixture begins to come together, adding more water, a tablespoon at a time, until the dough holds together when squeezed gently. Remove from the bowl; form the dough into a disc, wrap it in plastic wrap, and let it rest in the refrigerator while preparing the filling (about 30 minutes).

MAKE THE FILLING:

2. Cook the pancetta in a large skillet over medium–low heat to render some of the fat, about 10 minutes. Remove with a slotted spoon, blot on paper towels, and set aside. Add the onion to the pan and cook, stirring, over medium–low heat for 2–3 minutes. Stir in the mushrooms; raise the heat to medium and cook, stirring, another 2 minutes, until the mushrooms have softened. Reduce the heat to low, cover, and continue cooking, stirring occasionally, for another 5 minutes.

3. Meanwhile, chop the chard stems into small pieces and coarsely chop the leaves. Chop the kale leaves. Add the chard stems and kale to the onions, adding more oil if needed to prevent them from sticking. Cook, stirring, over medium heat for 2–3 minutes, then stir in the chard leaves. Cook for 1–2 minutes, then reduce the heat to low; cover and cook until the greens are wilted and tender, adding water as needed and stirring from time to time. Season to taste with salt and freshly ground pepper, and set aside.

4. Remove the pastry from the refrigerator and roll it out on a lightly floured board into a 16-inch circle. Carefully fit the pastry into a 9- x 3-inch spring-form pan, allowing the edges to drape over the sides. Lay the Asiago in the bottom of the pan.

5. Preheat your oven to 375°F.

6. In a medium bowl, whisk the 2 eggs together. Add the pancetta, cooked greens, and pine nuts; mix thoroughly. Pour and scrape the filling into the pastry-lined pan and spread evenly. Carefully bring the sides of the pastry up and fold over the top toward the center; the center of the torta will be exposed. Whisk the egg yolk in a small bowl and brush over the exposed pastry, being careful not to drip the egg down the edges of the pan or it will stick. Bake for 45 minutes, or until the pastry is a deep golden color.

7. Remove the torta from the oven, allow it to rest for 5 minutes, then loosen it from the sides of the pan and remove. Let it cool on a rack for another 10 minutes, then carefully slide it onto a serving plate and serve.

Gnocchi with Chicken Livers, Peas & Lardons

SERVES 4

In this rustic dish, gnocchi—Italian potato dumplings—and chicken livers and lardons are accented by bright green peas. It's a variation on the liver-and-bacon combination. It takes minutes to prepare if you buy ready-to-cook potato dumplings and boil them while cooking the chicken livers. Be sure to stop cooking the livers when they are still rosy in the center so they don't become dry. I use subtly smoked slab bacon or even pancetta for this. If you prefer, substitute 5 ounces of baby spinach leaves for the peas, stirring them into the chicken livers before combining them with the gnocchi.

1. In a very large, heavy skillet, cook the bacon over medium–high heat until the pieces are crisp and browned on all sides but still moist, about 6 minutes, stirring often. Remove them with a slotted spoon and blot on paper towels. Leave 2 tablespoons of the bacon fat in the pan. Reserve the remaining fat.

2. While the bacon cooks, bring a large pot of salted water to a boil. Add the gnocchi in batches and cook until they rise to the surface; cook 1 minute more, then drain well in large strainer; return them to the pan and toss with a little reserved bacon fat to prevent them from sticking together. It will take about 6–8 minutes for frozen gnocchi.

3. Meanwhile, heat the bacon fat over medium–high heat. Add the shallot and cook until wilted, about 1 minute, then stir in the chicken livers and cook until golden brown but still pale pink in the center, chopping them into coarse pieces with a wooden spatula. Stir in the peas and parsley, and season to taste with salt and pepper.

4. Stir in the bacon and vinegar. Add the gnocchi to the pan with the chicken livers and cook until heated through. Taste to adjust seasonings, then serve in flat soup bowls garnished with a sprinkle of Parmigiano-Reggiano.

½ pound slab bacon, rind removed, cut into 1- x ½- x ½-inch pieces

1 pound fresh or frozen gnocchi

1 large shallot, peeled and chopped

12 ounces chicken livers, cleaned with veins removed

1 cup frozen petite peas, defrosted

1 tablespoon chopped flat-leaf parsley

Coarse salt and freshly ground black pepper

2–3 teaspoons sherry or red wine vinegar

Freshly grated Parmigiano-Reggiano cheese

NOTE:

My friend Margret Kremenezky says that in Bavaria, Germany, *speck knödel*—dumplings made with white bread, chopped onion, parsley, finely chopped cooked bacon, milk, eggs, salt, and flour—are popular. The dumplings are gently boiled in salted water and then fried until crisp. "Speck" is the German word for a kind of bacon (see Baconology on page 9).

Spaghetti Carbonara

1 pound perciatelli or other thick
  spaghetti

2 tablespoons extra-virgin olive oil

⅓ pound lean slab bacon with rind
  removed, cut into ¼-inch cubes

1 medium yellow onion, chopped

2–3 large cloves garlic, thinly sliced

¼ cup dry white wine

½ cup light or heavy cream

2 eggs

1½ cups (4 ounces) freshly grated
  Parmigiano-Reggiano cheese

Coarse sea salt and coarsely ground
  black pepper

This beloved, classic Italian pasta dish is quick and easy to make. While the pasta boils, the sauce is prepared in a large skillet. The eggs, combined with cream and grated cheese, cook when tossed over the hot pasta. If you're concerned about raw eggs, or want to cut down on cholesterol, you can use pasteurized egg, egg whites, or egg substitute in this recipe. Some people—especially Romans—prefer to use Pecorino Romano rather than Parmigiano-Reggiano in this dish. (They also claim the dish originated in that city, but its roots are obscure.) The choice is yours, but if you do side with the Romans, note that Pecorino is far saltier, so you probably won't want to add any salt to the sauce.

1. Bring a large pot of salted water to a boil, add the pasta, and cook according to the package directions until al dente, about 11–12 minutes.

2. While the pasta cooks, heat the olive oil in a large, deep skillet over medium heat. Add the bacon and onion; cook until the bacon is lightly browned on all sides but still moist in the center, about 6–7 minutes. Stir in the garlic and cook for 1 minute. Pour in the wine and boil until reduced by half. Leave over low heat.

3. While the bacon is cooking, beat the cream, eggs, Parmigiano-Reggiano, a pinch of salt, and plenty of black pepper together in a bowl.

4. Drain the pasta well and immediately turn it into the pan with the bacon, then quickly stir in the cream-egg-cheese mixture, tossing to coat well. Taste to adjust seasonings, and serve immediately.

IDEA:

My former neighbor, Ed Giobbi, a cookbook author and prolific artist, suggests a more contemporary version of spaghetti carbonara. He uses just the beaten egg whites and adds blanched cauliflower florets to the pan to sauté with the bacon.

Nicole's Carbonara

Spaghetti carbonara made with turkey bacon has long been a favorite of my daughter Nicole because she doesn't eat red meat. One advantage of turkey bacon is that it takes just minutes to warm up. Because there is virtually no fat to melt and impart flavor, I use fragrant extra-virgin olive oil to boost the taste. I also like the addition of toasted pine nuts.

1. Bring a large pot of salted water to a boil. Add the pasta and cook it according to the package directions, about 11 minutes, or until al dente.

2. Beat the eggs and parsley together in a large, flat bowl. Set aside.

3. While the pasta is cooking, heat the olive oil in a large, deep skillet over medium–high heat. Add the onion and cook until golden, 3–4 minutes. Stir in the garlic, cook 30 seconds, then add the bacon. Pour in the wine, stirring up any browned cooking bits, and cook until the liquid has almost evaporated. Keep warm on low heat.

4. Drain the pasta and immediately turn it into the pot with the onions and bacon. Toss well, then turn into the bowl with the eggs, tossing to coat the pasta with eggs. Add the pine nuts, Parmigiano-Reggiano, and salt and pepper to taste. Toss well and serve at once.

½ pound uncooked perciatelli or other thick spaghetti

2 large eggs

2 tablespoons finely chopped flat-leaf parsley

2 tablespoons fragrant extra-virgin olive oil

1 small onion, finely chopped

1 large clove garlic, minced

3 ounces thick-sliced turkey bacon, cut into ½-inch squares

⅓ cup dry white wine

2 tablespoons pine nuts, toasted

½ cup freshly grated Parmigiano-Reggiano cheese

Salt and plenty of coarsely ground black pepper

NOTE:
Perciatelli is a hollow spaghetti that is somewhat thicker than bucatini.

Don Vittorio's Rigatoni with Tomato-Vodka Sauce

2 tablespoons unsalted butter

12 slices bacon, cut crosswise into ¼-inch pieces

¾ cup vodka

3 cups canned tomato sauce

½ cup heavy cream

Coarsely ground black pepper

1½ pounds dry rigatoni, ziti, or penne

2–3 tablespoons chopped fresh basil

Grated Parmigiano-Reggiano cheese

Dinner at the home of friends Vic and Jinny Alasio is always a copious and delicious event. One of Vic's staples is this pasta sauce served over ziti, penne rigate, or rigatoni (Vic's favorite). He says that while you can use pancetta or even prosciutto, he thinks bacon tastes the best.

Some chefs like to finish the sauce with the butter, but Don Vittorio— the name we call Vic when he is the maestro chef for the evening—likes to cook the bacon in butter; he says the combination adds a great flavor to the sauce. Serve with garlic bread and a little salad.

1. Melt the butter in a large, deep skillet over medium–high heat. Add the bacon and cook over medium heat until almost crisp.

2. Remove the pan from the stove and pour in the vodka. Carefully ignite the liquid and allow the alcohol to burn off.

3. Return the skillet to the heat and stir in the tomato sauce. Stir in the cream and season liberally with pepper. Keep warm.

4. Cook the pasta in a large pot of salted water until al dente. Drain and transfer to a large platter. Ladle the sauce over the pasta, garnish with basil, toss to blend, and serve. Pass the cheese at the table.

Macattacaroni

½ pound dry elbow macaroni

8 slices thick-sliced bacon, cut cross-wise into 1-inch pieces

1 medium yellow onion, diced

3 tablespoons butter

3 tablespoons flour

2½ cups milk

1 teaspoon Hungarian paprika

1 teaspoon salt or to taste

Freshly ground black pepper

1 large egg

3 cups shredded sharp Cheddar cheese

½ cup grated Parmigiano-Reggiano cheese

¼ cup Panko or coarsely ground dried bread crumbs

When I was growing up, my mom made the most wonderful macaroni-and-cheese casserole. It was a basic cream sauce with onion, paprika, and loads of Tillamook or sharp Cheddar cheese mixed with the pasta. My siblings and I loved the crunchy browned cheese topping.

Mom baked it in a deep cast-iron skillet she got as a wedding present. For this version, I use a 10-inch-wide ceramic quiche dish because making it wider than deeper creates lots of crunchies. When I added bacon to the filling and Parmesan cheese to the topping, our friends simply attacked that mac with a vengeance. Panko are dried bread crumbs that are larger than commercial bread crumbs. You can find them at Asian and specialty grocery stores.

1. Preheat your oven to 350°F.

2. Bring a large pot of salted water to a boil. Add the pasta and cook it until al dente, about 8 minutes; drain and set aside.

3. Meanwhile, cook the bacon in a large skillet over medium–high heat until the fat begins to melt and covers the bottom of the pan. Stir in the onion and continue cooking until the bacon is crisp and the onions are golden brown, stirring often. Set aside.

4. In a large saucepan, melt the butter over medium–high heat. Whisk in the flour and cook over medium heat until the mixture begins to color slightly and is completely smooth, stirring constantly. Whisk in the milk, paprika, salt, and plenty of black pepper. Reduce the heat and simmer for 10 minutes.

5. Beat the egg in a bowl. Whisk ½ cup of the white sauce into the egg to raise the temperature, then whisk the mixture into the pot with the sauce. Stir 2 cups of the cheese into sauce until melted. Season with salt and pepper. Stir the macaroni and onion-bacon mixture into the sauce and scrape into a 10-inch quiche dish or 2-quart casserole dish. Put the casserole on a baking sheet.

6. Combine the remaining 1 cup Cheddar, the Parmigiano-Reggiano, and the Panko crumbs in a bowl. Spoon the topping over the macaroni and bake for 30 minutes until the top is lightly browned. If it is not browned enough, turn the broiler on and cook for 3–4 minutes longer, watching carefully that it doesn't burn. Remove the casserole and let it cool for 5 minutes before serving.

NOTE:

You could also add chopped marinated artichokes and/or oil-cured sun-dried tomatoes to this. It's not my mother's style, but I love it. A few very thin slices of fresh tomato might also be nice arranged under the topping.

Song to Bacon

Consumer groups have gone and taken
Some of the savor out of bacon.
Protein-per-penny in bacon, they say,
Equals needles-per-square-inch of hay.
Well, I know, after cooking all
That's left to eat is mighty small
(You also get a lot of lossage
In life, romance, and country sausage),
And I will vote for making it cheaper,
Wider, longer, leaner, deeper,
But let's not throw the baby, please,
Out with the (visual rhyme here) grease.
There's nothing crumbles like bacon still,
And I don't think there ever will
Be anything, whate'er you use
For meat, that chews like bacon chews.
And also: I wish these groups would tell
Me whether they counted in the smell.
The smell of it cooking's worth $2.10 a pound.
And howbout the sound?

—Roy Blount

Risotto with Shrimp, Asparagus & Pancetta

SERVES 2 AS A MAIN COURSE; 4 AS A FIRST COURSE

In this risotto, small shrimp and tender asparagus are stirred into slowly simmered Arborio rice perfumed with pancetta and fresh tarragon. Serve this as a main course or smaller first course. Either way, you may swoon with pleasure. Allowing the shrimp to cook in the almost-finished risotto keeps them succulent and tasty.

1. Fill a large, deep skillet with salted water and bring to a boil. Add the asparagus and cook it until just tender, about 5–6 minutes; drain, shock under cold water, and drain again. Cut crosswise into ¾-inch pieces, wrap in paper towels, and set aside. Reserve 4 tips for a final garnish.

2. Heat the olive oil in a large skillet over medium heat. Add the onions and sauté until golden. Stir in the rice, turning it to coat the grains with oil, and continue cooking until the rice begins to turn opaque, 1–2 minutes. Pour in the wine and cook until the liquid almost evaporates, stirring constantly.

3. Begin adding the simmering stock to the rice, ½ cup at a time, constantly stirring and waiting until the liquid is absorbed before adding more. Cook until the rice is al dente, about 20–25 minutes.

4. Before adding the last ½ cup of stock, stir in the shrimp and pancetta. Cook until the shrimp turn pink. Once the shrimp are cooked, stir in the reserved asparagus, cook 1–2 minutes, then stir in the cream and tarragon. Season to taste with salt and pepper. Serve at once on heated plates. Garnish with asparagus tips.

½ pound thin young asparagus, woody ends snapped off

2 tablespoons olive oil

⅓ cup finely chopped onion

½ cup Arborio rice

¼ cup dry white wine

2 cups low-sodium chicken stock, heated

½ pound small shrimp, peeled and deveined

2 ounces thinly sliced pancetta, finely chopped

2 tablespoons heavy cream

1 tablespoon finely chopped fresh tarragon leaves *or* 1 teaspoon dried leaves

Salt and freshly ground black pepper

Blazin' Baked Beans

SERVES 12

2 pounds pea or navy beans, rinsed and picked over

1 tablespoon salt or to taste

½ pound lean, hickory-smoked slab bacon with rind removed, finely diced

2 tablespoons bacon fat or vegetable oil

1½ cups yellow onions, chopped

2 chipotle chiles in adobo sauce, finely chopped

⅓ cup Dijon mustard

⅓ cup firmly packed dark brown sugar

1 (18-ounce) jar high-quality smoky barbecue sauce

Boiling water

If you're a fan of baked beans with a little heat, this easy-to-make version scented with chipotle chiles in adobo sauce will surely excite your taste buds. Smoked bacon helps reinforce the barbecue flavors. Supermarkets now sell lots of prepared barbecue sauces, many by famous chefs. Read the labels and choose one that doesn't include a lot of artificial ingredients and preservatives. Serve these beans with Rise 'n' Shine Mexican Cornbread (page 19).

1. Put the beans in a large, heavy pot and add enough water to cover. Bring the water to a boil for 3 minutes, then turn off the heat, cover the pot, and let it stand 1 hour. Drain the beans. Cover again with water, add the salt, and bring to a boil for 5 minutes, then reduce the heat, cover, and simmer for 30 minutes longer. Remove the pot from the heat and let the beans stand in their cooking liquid until cool.

2. Meanwhile, preheat your oven to 250°F.

3. Sauté the bacon in a large skillet over medium heat until lightly browned, turning often. Remove, blot on paper towels, and set aside. Reserve 2 tablespoons of the bacon fat in the skillet and heat over medium–high heat. Add the onions and sauté them until golden brown. Set aside.

5. Drain the beans and combine them with the bacon, onions, chipotle chiles, mustard, brown sugar, and barbecue sauce in a large casserole. Add enough boiling water to cover the beans, then cover the casserole, and bake for 4 hours. Uncover the casserole for last 30 minutes of cooking time, or until the liquid is reduced and the beans are very tender. Taste to adjust the seasonings, adding salt if needed. Let stand 15 minutes before serving.

NOTE:

Lee Hefter, executive chef/managing partner of the Wolfgang Puck Fine Dining Group, including the Spago restaurants in Los Angeles, Tokyo, Las Vegas, Mexico City, and Chicago, loves bacon for its versatility and smoky flavors. He has used it since the first Spago opened in Hollywood, in 1982.

"Some of my dishes include wrapping whole slices of slab bacon around loins of rabbit and cooking them like confit of duck. I love to braise bacon with beans. I also make a warm vinaigrette with rendered bacon fat for a wild mushroom salad served with crisp bacon on top."

Moros y Cristianos (Black Beans & Rice)

SERVES 6-8

Black beans and rice are a staple in many Latin kitchens. This version is one of the best side dishes I've ever eaten. It is based on a recipe of Maximo Tejada from the Dominican Republic. He's the talented chef of Lucy's Latin Kitchen in New York City. Eat it with pulled pork—a natural combination—and also with grilled salmon or barbecued chicken.

1. In a large pot, heat the oil over medium heat. Add about three-quarters of the bacon, the bell peppers, onion, garlic, and cumin and sauté 5–7 minutes. Stir in the tomatoes, black beans, and chicken stock and simmer for about 5 minutes, stirring frequently, until heated through.

2. Add the rice and water, cover, and cook over medium–low heat for 20 minutes, or until the rice is tender, stirring occasionally. Remove the cover, raise the heat, and boil until the liquid is almost absorbed, stirring occasionally.

3. Meanwhile, sauté the remaining ¼ cup bacon in a skillet until lightly browned on all sides but still moist in the center. When the rice is tender, stir the bacon into the pan, season to taste with salt and pepper, and cook a few minutes longer, stirring often. Before serving, add the cilantro and taste to adjust seasonings.

2 tablespoons olive oil

7 slices thick-sliced bacon, cut into ¼-inch cubes

½ cup each seeded and diced red and green bell peppers

1 medium onion, diced

2 garlic cloves, crushed

1 tablespoon ground cumin

1 (14½-ounce) can diced tomatoes, drained

4 cups cooked black beans

1 cup chicken stock

1 cup long-grained white rice

2 cups water

Salt and freshly ground black pepper

½ cup chopped cilantro, to garnish

IDEA:

Beans and bacon are such a compatible duo. They are partners in Blazin' Baked Beans (page 144). Bacon also loves rice. For a simple side dish, add small cubes of partially cooked bacon to boiled rice that is almost cooked and let them finish cooking together. Stir in toasted pine nuts and chopped parsley, and serve.

Life expectancy would grow by leaps and bounds if green vegetables smelled as good as bacon. —GARY LARSON, author of *The Far Side*

vegetable side dishes

Stir-Fried Brussels Sprouts, Shiitakes & Scallions

SERVES 4

4 slices bacon, cut into ¼" cubes

10 ounces Brussels sprouts, trimmed and sliced

3 ounces shiitake or oyster mushrooms, wiped, stems removed and discarded, cut into thick slices

8 scallions, including most of green parts, trimmed and sliced

2 tablespoons medium sherry

1½ tablespoons soy sauce

1 tablespoon toasted sesame oil

Pinch red pepper flakes

Here's the perfect antidote for people who say they loathe Brussels sprouts. Stir-fried bright green ribbons of sprouts marry wonderfully with sliced shiitake mushrooms, scallions, and bacon. The fragrance and crisp-tender texture are fresh and exciting. It's a long way from the intolerably sulphurous smell of over-boiled sprouts. Serve whenever you want to add a lot of color and taste to your dinner plate.

1. In a large wok, heat the bacon over medium heat until the fat covers the bottom of the pan, 2–3 minutes. Add the Brussels sprouts and stir-fry until they are bright green, 2–3 minutes, stirring constantly. Stir in the shiitakes and scallions and stir-fry for 3 minutes more.

2. Add the sherry and soy sauce, raise the heat to high, and cook for 2 minutes longer, stirring often. Stir in the sesame oil and pepper flakes, and serve.

Rapini with Pine Nuts & Currants

SERVES 4-6

1 pound rapini, coarse stems removed
  and discarded, roughly chopped

4 slices thick-sliced bacon, cut in
  ½-inch pieces

2 tablespoons extra-virgin olive oil

2 large cloves garlic, sliced

3 tablespoons dried currants (optional)

4 tablespoons pine nuts, lightly toasted

Salt and freshly ground black pepper

I simply love rapini's bitter taste. Bob doesn't. But in combination with bacon, pine nuts, and currants, we both agree that this is a very appealing vegetable side dish. Using currants with bitter greens is reminiscent of Sicilian and Middle Eastern dishes. They add a seductively complex flavor to the dish. But leave them out if you prefer. Rapini is also known as broccoli rabe.

1. Bring a large pot of salted water to a boil. Add the rapini and cook until wilted, about 3–4 minutes. Drain well and set aside.

2. In the same pot, heat the bacon and olive oil over medium–high heat. Cook until the bacon separates and begins to brown, about 2 minutes. Add the garlic and cook 1 minute more.

3. Return the rapini to the pot and cook over low heat for 5–6 minutes, shaking the pan often. Add the currants, if using, and the pine nuts. Season to taste with salt and plenty of pepper. Serve at once, or leave over low heat for up to 1 hour.

NOTE:
Choose the variety and flavor of bacon according to the other ingredients in the dish and your own preferences. For bitter greens, assertive-tasting bacon is preferable. It might be double-smoked or pepper-crusted.

Green Pea & Pancetta Packets

SERVES 4

1 ounce pancetta (about ¼ cup), finely chopped

1 small onion, finely chopped

4 tablespoons unsalted butter

1 (10-ounce) package frozen petite peas, defrosted and blotted dry on paper towels

⅓ cup whole-milk ricotta cheese

2 tablespoons finely chopped chives + chives to garnish

Salt and freshly ground black pepper

2 sheets phyllo, defrosted according to package directions

Tender little green peas scented with pancetta and onions, wrapped inside phyllo, dress up Crispy Oven-Roasted Chicken (page 120), broiled salmon, or any meal where you want a special vegetable dish.

1. Cook the pancetta in a medium skillet over medium–low heat for 2 minutes. Stir in the chopped onion and cook until translucent and tender, 2–3 minutes. Add 2 tablespoons butter and the peas, cover, and cook gently for 3 minutes. Remove from heat, then scrape the mixture into a bowl and let cool. Stir in the ricotta and chives; season to taste with salt and pepper.

2. Preheat your oven to 375°F. Lightly grease a baking sheet.

3. Melt the remaining butter. Lay a sheet of phyllo horizontally on a clean workspace, brush lightly with butter, fold in half horizontally, then cut in half vertically to make two rectangles each measuring 8 inches wide by 7 inches high. Spoon one-fourth of the pea mixture into the center of each rectangle leaving a ¾" border on either side. Fold the bottom third of the phyllo over the peas, turn in both sides, and roll up into a packet measuring about 4 x 3 inches. Put the packet on the baking sheet and brush the top with butter. Repeat with the remaining phyllo and peas.

4. Transfer to oven and bake until the tops are golden brown and crisp, about 25 minutes. Remove from the oven, sprinkle a few chives on top of each packet, and serve at once.

NOTE:

While working with phyllo, cover the unused portion with a damp cloth or towel to prevent it from drying out.

Glazed Pearl Onions

SERVES 4-6

These onions are so delicious and easy, you'll find everyone will love them—including the chef. Peeling a lot of tiny pearl onions takes a lot of time. To speed up the preparation I use the frozen ones—especially at holidays when I'm called upon to cook for 12 to 20. If you remove only the excess ice from the onions they hold their shape better. I love maple-cured or applewood-smoked bacon in this recipe.

4 ounces slab bacon with rind removed, cut into ½-inch cubes

1 (16-ounce) package frozen pearl onions

3 tablespoons sugar

1½ cups beef stock

½ teaspoon fresh thyme leaves or ¼ teaspoon dried leaves

3–4 tablespoons red wine vinegar

Salt and freshly ground pepper

1. Heat the bacon in a large, heavy skillet over medium–high heat and cook until the pieces are browned on all sides, turning them often. Remove with a slotted spoon and blot on paper towels. Discard all but 2 tablespoons of the bacon fat.

2. Rinse the onions in a strainer to separate them and remove the extra ice. Blot them on paper towels. Heat the bacon fat over high heat, add the onions and sugar, and cook for 5 minutes, shaking the pan often, until the onions are lightly colored. Add the beef stock and thyme, adjust the heat to medium–high, and continue cooking until the liquid is almost completely evaporated, about 20–25 minutes, stirring often. Stir in the reserved bacon and vinegar, cook for 30 seconds, season to taste with salt and pepper, and serve.

IDEA:

Reserve large pieces of rind cut from slab bacon to use in flavoring soups or to wrap around grilled fish or chicken during cooking. See Barbecued Barramundi on page 99.

Sautéed Green Beans, Shallots & Bacon

SERVES 4-6

A delicious side dish good enough to serve at your fanciest meals or with a simple grilled chicken. The beans, shallots, and bacon may be cooked ahead and then finished at the last minute.

1 pound green beans, stem-end trimmed

4 slices thick-sliced bacon

5 ounces shallots, thinly sliced

Salt and freshly ground black pepper

1. Bring a large pot of salted water to a boil, add the beans, and cook until crisp-tender. Drain, shock under cold water, and blot dry on paper towels.

2. Cook the bacon in a heavy skillet over medium heat until very crisp. Remove, blot on paper towels, then crumble and set aside. Reserve the bacon fat.

3. Heat the bacon fat until hot over medium heat. Add the shallots and sauté them until crisp and golden brown, 6–8 minutes, stirring often; remove them with a slotted spoon and set aside. Add the green beans to the pan and, over high heat, sauté them for 2–3 minutes, shaking the pan often. Stir in the reserved bacon and shallots, and cook until heated through. Season to taste with salt and pepper, and serve.

NOTE:

To retain a more intense bacon flavor and firmer texture, add cooked bacon toward the end of the cooking time.

Wild Mushroom Ragoût on Wild Rice Pancakes

SERVES 4

2 ounces dried wild mushrooms

4 slices thick-sliced bacon, cut into small pieces

½ cup finely chopped shallots

½ cup tawny port

Salt and freshly ground black pepper to taste

2 tablespoons minced flat-leaf parsley

Luscious wild mushroom ragoût atop earthy wild rice pancakes will dress up even the simplest roast or grilled bird. Any kind of mushroom can be used. Applewood-smoked bacon or pepper-crusted bacon would be good choices to partner with the other ingredients.

1. In a small bowl, pour boiling water over the mushrooms and soak them until soft, about 20–30 minutes. Strain the mushroom soaking liquid through a fine sieve lined with a dampened paper towel, and reserve the liquid. Discard coarse stems and remove any grit from the mushrooms. Transfer the soaking liquid to a small saucepan and boil to reduce it to about ½ cup.

2. Cook the bacon until crisp, remove with a slotted spoon, and drain on paper towels. Reserve 2 teaspoons of the fat, and heat it in a saucepan over medium heat. Add the shallots and sauté them until limp and beginning to brown, 1½ minutes. Stir in the port, reduced soaking liquid, and mushrooms, and bring the liquid to a boil over high heat. Continue cooking until the liquid has almost completely evaporated. Season with salt and a liberal amount of pepper. Stir in the parsley and bacon and leave the pan on low heat, partially covered, until the pancakes are ready.

WILD RICE PANCAKES

½ cup flour

¼ cup buckwheat flour

1 teaspoon baking powder

¼ teaspoon salt or to taste

Generous pinch freshly ground black pepper

¼ cup finely chopped pecans

1 egg

1 cup low-fat milk

1 cup cooked wild rice

1–2 tablespoons oil

WILD RICE PANCAKES

1. Combine the flours, baking powder, salt, pepper, and pecans in a bowl. Beat the egg and milk together, then stir into the dry ingredients until blended. Stir in the wild rice. Preheat the oven to warm.

2. Heat a large, non-stick skillet over medium–high heat. Add 1 tablespoon oil and, when hot, pour in ¼ cup of batter for each 3½-inch pancake. Cook until bubbles form on the surface and the underside is golden brown when lifted with a spatula, about 1½–2 minutes. Turn and cook the second side until golden brown, 1½ minutes. Transfer to a warm oven and continue until all the pancakes are cooked. Serve immediately, topped with the mushroom ragoût.

Yams with Pecan, Marshmallow & Bacon Streusel

Here's an indulgence to prepare for a crowd or just for you (adjusting the quantity accordingly). Bacon adds a delightful complement to the other flavors and textures. While yams and sweet potatoes are both root vegetables, they are not from the same plant. However, the two tubers are used interchangably. Yams are actually sweeter and have a moister texture.

1. Preheat your oven to 400°F. Butter a 10-inch round Pyrex pie plate or a shallow 6-cup casserole.

2. Bake the yams until a knife inserted in the centers goes in easily, about 45–50 minutes. Remove the yams from the oven; cut them in half lengthwise, remove the flesh, and mash. Transfer the mashed yams to the prepared baking dish.

3. While the yams are baking, cut the 6 tablespoons butter, brown sugar, and flour together in a large bowl using two knives until the mixture is crumbly. In another bowl, blend the cinnamon, salt, pecans, marshmallows, and bacon; toss gently with the butter-sugar mixture. Sprinkle the topping over the mashed potatoes; then put the dish, uncovered, in the oven and bake until the topping is bubbly and brown, about 20 minutes. Remove from the oven and serve.

Unsalted butter to grease baking dish

6 large yams or sweet potatoes, scrubbed and pricked with a fork

6 tablespoons unsalted butter, at room temperature

1/3 cup firmly-packed light brown sugar

1/3 cup flour

1/8 teaspoon ground cinnamon

1/4 teaspoon salt

1 cup coarsely chopped pecans, lightly toasted

1 cup miniature marshmallows

6 slices bacon, cooked until very crisp, blotted on paper towels and crumbled

Zucchini Gratin with Tomato Coulis

SERVES 8

FOR THE ZUCCHINI GRATIN:

1 tablespoon unsalted butter

8 slices bacon, cut crosswise into 1-inch pieces

3 medium zucchini, washed and cut crosswise into ¼-inch slices

2 large shallots, finely chopped

2 eggs

½ cup whole milk

½ cup freshly grated Parmigiano-Reggiano cheese

⅓ cup cooked white rice

¼ teaspoon freshly grated nutmeg

Salt and freshly ground black pepper

Tomato Coulis (recipe follows)

FOR THE TOMATO COULIS:

3 firm, ripe tomatoes

½ teaspoon salt or to taste

Freshly ground black pepper

½ teaspoon sugar

1 tablespoon freshly chopped mint or basil

A versatile late-summer dish to serve warm or at room temperature, this gratin is reminiscent of the lovely summer dishes I tasted in the south of France where the vegetables come fresh from the garden. It is a delightful accompaniment to leg of lamb or roast chicken.

MAKE THE ZUCCHINI GRATIN:

1. Preheat your oven to 350°F. Grease an 8-inch square baking dish with butter. Set aside.

2. Cook the bacon in a large, heavy skillet until crisp; remove and blot on paper towels. Scatter the bacon in the baking dish.

3. Discard all but 2 tablespoons of fat from the pan. Heat the fat over medium–high heat. Stir in the zucchini and sauté until it is wilted and lightly colored, about 5–7 minutes, shaking the pan often. Reduce the heat to medium, stir in the shallots, and cook for 1½ minutes longer, or until the shallots are wilted.

4. In a large bowl, beat the eggs and milk together. Add the zucchini mixture, half the cheese, the rice, nutmeg, and salt and pepper to taste. Pour the mixture into the prepared baking dish, smooth the top, and sprinkle with the remaining cheese. Bake until a knife inserted in the center of the gratin comes out clean, about 20 minutes.

5. Meanwhile, prepare the Tomato Coulis (see facing page). Remove the gratin from the oven and cool for at least 10 minutes. Cut into squares and serve with Tomato Coulis ladled over the top.

PREPARE THE TOMATO COULIS:

1. Drop the tomatoes in a saucepan of boiling water for about 20–30 seconds. Remove them with a slotted spoon and use a sharp paring knife to peel away the skin. Cut the peeled tomatoes in half horizontally. With the rounded side in the palm of your hand, squeeze gently to extract the seeds.

2. Process the tomatoes, salt, pepper, and sugar in a food processor. The purée can be very smooth or chunky, depending on the texture you want. Add the mint or basil and taste to adjust the seasonings, if necessary.

Our Favorite Creamed Spinach

SERVES 8

2 (10-ounce) packages frozen leaf or chopped spinach *or* 2½ pounds fresh spinach, washed and stems removed

Salt

8 slices bacon, cut crosswise into ½-inch-wide pieces

1 large onion, finely chopped

2 tablespoons unsalted butter

2 tablespoons flour

1 cup milk

½ teaspoon paprika

⅛ teaspoon cayenne pepper

Generous pinch freshly grated nutmeg

Freshly ground black pepper to taste

I'm always amazed at how many people love well-seasoned creamed spinach. I've served this version for years, and the hint of bacon always draws raves. Frozen spinach is an excellent alternative to the fresh vegetable.

1. In a medium saucepan, cook the spinach according to the package directions, then drain well, squeezing out as much moisture as you can, and set aside. Or shake most of the water from the fresh spinach, combine it with ½ teaspoon salt in a large, deep saucepan, cover, and cook until tender, about 5–7 minutes. Drain well in a strainer, pressing on the spinach with a wooden spoon to extract as much moisture as possible.

2. Cook the bacon in a large skillet over medium–high heat until crisp; remove from the pan with a slotted spoon and blot on paper towels. Discard all but 2 tablespoons of the fat (or reserve it for another purpose). Add the onion and sauté until it is lightly colored, about 6–7 minutes. Stir in the reserved spinach and bacon, and mix well.

3. Melt the butter in a small saucepan. Add the flour and cook over medium–low heat for a few minutes until it is pale yellow, stirring with a wooden spoon. Add the milk all at once and whisk until the mixture is smooth and thick. Add the paprika, cayenne, and nutmeg; scrape the white sauce into the spinach-onion mixture and stir to blend; season with salt and pepper to taste, and serve.

NOTE:

You can sauté many foods in bacon fat, including vegetables. However, in some cases, as above, butter adds a certain richness and nutty flavor to the base of the white sauce, so it is a better choice here.

Ella Simmerer's German Potato Salad

SERVES AT LEAST 8-10

German-style potato salad probably came to America with immigrants known as Pennsylvania Dutch (which, in reality, was a mispronunciation of the word deutsch, *or German). Bob grew up with this kind of salad in Ohio, where many of his relatives had moved. This is an old family recipe from one of them.*

1. Cook the bacon in a large, heavy skillet over medium–high heat until crisp but still moist in the center. Remove with a slotted spoon and blot on paper towels. Reserve about 3 tablespoons of the fat in the skillet.

2. In a large pot, cover the whole potatoes with cold water; bring to a boil and cook until the potatoes are just tender when a knife is inserted into the center, about 20–23 minutes. Drain, and when the potatoes are cool enough to handle, cut them into thin slices.

3. Add the vinegar, sugar, and onion to the bacon skillet and bring to a simmer; add the potatoes, eggs, and bacon, turn, and cook 5–10 minutes longer. Season to taste with salt and pepper. Serve warm.

2 pounds slab bacon with rind removed, cut into ½-inch cubes

10 medium potatoes (about 3½ pounds), peeled

1¾ cups white vinegar

2 tablespoons sugar

1 large onion, chopped

10 eggs, hard-cooked and sliced

Salt and freshly ground black pepper

Three-Potato–Bacon Salad

1½ pounds mixed very small red, yellow, and blue potatoes, washed

Coarse salt

½ cup mayonnaise

½–1 tablespoon curry paste, hot or mild to taste; *or* 2–3 teaspoons curry powder (optional)

6 ounces double-smoked slab bacon with rind removed, cut into ½-inch cubes

½ cup finely chopped shallots

¼ cup dry white wine

½ cup chopped celery

½ cup chopped cilantro

Freshly ground black pepper

Potato salad has long been a classic for picnics: it's great casual fare. This updated interpretation would also be welcome with grilled cheese sandwiches, a simple roast chicken, or with grilled sausages served at home. If you cannot find yellow potatoes, substitute peeled, diced sweet potatoes.

1. Put the potatoes in a medium-sized saucepan and cover them with cold water. Add a generous sprinkle of salt and bring the water to a boil. Cook for about 6 minutes, or until a knife inserted into a potato goes in with little resistance. (Cook larger potatoes to the same degree of doneness.) Drain, cover the pan with a dishcloth and lid, and let cool. Cut the cooled potatoes into ½-inch slices and put them into a large bowl.

2. Combine the mayonnaise and curry paste, and toss with the potatoes.

3. Cook the bacon in a large skillet over medium heat until browned on all sides but still moist in the center, about 5–6 minutes. Transfer with a slotted spoon to the bowl with the potatoes. Discard all but 1 tablespoon of the bacon fat, add the shallots, and sauté them until wilted and golden. Pour in the wine and bring to a boil. Cook 30 seconds, then scrape the mixture into the bowl with the potatoes. Add the celery and cilantro; toss to blend, and season to taste with salt and pepper. Toss again and serve.

Bacon and desserts: from improbable to incomparable.

—GENE KOFKE, bacon bard

desserts

166

PECAN–BROWN SUGAR & BACON ICE CREAM

167

WHITE CHOCOLATE BACON CURLS

168

FRENCH APPLE TART WITH CHEDDAR CHEESE CRUST &
SWEET BRITTLE TOPPING

170

NUTMEG-SCENTED CANTALOUPE SHERBET
WITH BACON TUILES

Pecan–Brown Sugar & Bacon Ice Cream

MAKES 1½ QUARTS

3 cups heavy cream

1 cup milk

1¼ cups firmly packed dark brown sugar

4 egg yolks

1 cup chopped pecans

1 pound bacon, cooked until very crisp, blotted on paper towels and finely chopped (about ½ cup)

Here's a delicious surprise: tiny bits of salty bacon are a wonderful addition to this creamy dessert. Serve it with the hot caramel sauce on page 14, with or without the bacon added. Maple-cured or applewood-smoked bacon seem to be ideal choices here. You could also serve the Caramel-Bacon Sauce on page 14 over purchased butter pecan ice cream.

1. Combine the cream, milk, and sugar in a heavy saucepan and cook over medium–high heat until hot and the sugar is completely dissolved, stirring occasionally.

2. In a small bowl, beat the egg yolks until smooth. Slowly whisk in 1 cup of the hot cream-milk mixture. Return the yolk mixture to the saucepan, beating constantly. Cook over medium heat, stirring continuously, until the mixture coats the back of a wooden spoon, 6–8 minutes. Do not let it boil.

3. Strain the mixture into a clean bowl and let it cool completely. Stir in pecans and bacon and freeze in an ice cream maker according to manufacturer's directions. To showcase the ice cream's flavor, before serving, remove from freezer and let it soften slightly.

NOTE:

Salty bacon used judiciously with a sweet food accentuates its taste and makes the final experience more exciting.

White Chocolate Bacon Curls

SERVES ABOUT 8 AS
PART OF A COOKIE PLATE

6 ounces white chocolate

2 (1½-ounce) bags pork rinds

Sea salt and freshly ground black
pepper

Just as I was putting the finishing touches on this book, Bob and I dined at Compass, in New York City, where pastry chef Vera Tong served these incredible crunchies on a plate of cookies. Alternatively called pork rinds, pork skins, bacon curls, or chicharrones, after tasting the white chocolate coated curls, I bolted into the kitchen and asked for the recipe. Vera said the idea came to her in a dream. All dreams should be this sweet. If tightly covered, they will keep for 3 days in low humidity.

1. Heat 4 ounces of the white chocolate in a double boiler over barely simmering water. While the chocolate is melting, finely chop the remaining 2 ounces of chocolate. Once the chocolate is about three-quarters melted, remove the insert from the double boiler.

2. Add the chopped chocolate and stir vigorously. When the mixture is smooth, dip each pork rind into the chocolate and set out on wax paper to cool. While they are cooling, season the bacon curls liberally with salt and black pepper.

French Apple Tart with Cheddar Cheese Crust & Sweet Brittle Topping

SERVES 8-12

FOR CRUST:

1¼ cups flour

¼ teaspoon salt

2 ounces (about ¾ cup) shredded aged sharp Cheddar cheese

4 tablespoons chilled unsalted butter, cut into small cubes

4 tablespoons chilled bacon fat

4 tablespoons apple cider

FOR FILLING:

4 large Granny Smith apples

4 tablespoons unsalted butter

¼ cup + 1 tablespoon sugar

1 tablespoon lemon juice

¼ teaspoon ground cinnamon

Pinch salt

1 egg white, lightly beaten

1 cup sweetened applesauce

⅓ cup apricot preserves, heated and strained

2 slices bacon, cooked until crisp, blotted on paper towels and crumbled

1 ounce purchased almond or peanut brittle

A showstopper of a dessert that combines the best of traditional French baking with contemporary thinking. Who would have thought that crisp bacon and almond or peanut brittle would make the ultimate crunchy garnishing on a sweet apple tart? It does. Give it a try. I like maple-cured or applewood-smoked bacon for this recipe.

To gild the lily, you could serve Pecan–Brown Sugar & Bacon Ice Cream (page 166) on top.

PREPARE THE CRUST:

1. In a food processor, combine the flour, salt, and cheese and pulse until well blended. Add butter and bacon fat and pulse until mixture resembles coarse meal. Add apple cider and process just until mixture pulls into a ball. Remove, sprinkle with a little flour, wrap in plastic, and refrigerate for 1 hour.

2. Preheat your oven to 375°F.

3. Remove the pastry from the refrigerator and roll into a circle measuring about 14 inches in diameter and ⅛ inch thick. Transfer to an 11-inch French tart pan and trim the crust even with the edge of the pan. Prick the bottom generously with a fork. Smooth a piece of aluminum foil, shiny-side down, over the pastry, smoothing it against the edges. Fill with baking weights, dried beans, or rice, and bake on a cookie sheet until the sides of the shell look set, about 10 minutes. Remove the beans and foil, return the shell to the oven, and continue baking until the crust is firm and lightly colored, about 6 minutes. Remove and let cool on a rack. Turn the oven down to 350°F.

MAKE THE FILLING:

4. While the tart shell is baking, peel, core, and slice the apples into sixteenths. In a large skillet, melt the butter and add the apples. Cook 5 minutes, or until the apples are flexible, then remove them with a slotted spoon to a large bowl. Stir ¼ cup sugar, the lemon juice, cinnamon, and salt into the skillet and boil the liquid until it is reduced by half.

5. Once the tart shell cools, brush it with egg white. Spread the applesauce on the bottom of the crust. Place the apple slices in an overlapping pattern around the outside, then fill in the center, laying the slices in the opposite direction. Spread the reduced liquid over the apples and sprinkle on the remaining tablespoon of sugar. Bake until the apples are very tender, about 45 minutes. Remove the tart from the oven; slide off the sides of the tart pan, leaving the bottom under the tart. Brush the apples with the warm apricot preserves.

6. While the tart is baking, pulse the bacon and almond brittle in the food processor until fairly fine. After brushing the tart with the preserves, sprinkle the brittle crumbs around the outside edge of the tart. Let it set for at least 10 minutes before cutting into slices and serving.

Nutmeg-Scented Cantaloupe Sherbet with Bacon Tuiles

SERVES 8

FOR THE SHERBET:

1 large cantaloupe, peeled, seeded, and cut into chunks

2 tablespoons strained fresh lemon juice

½ cup superfine granulated sugar

½ teaspoon salt

1 teaspoon freshly grated nutmeg + additional nutmeg to garnish

3 cups cold milk

Prosciutto and cantaloupe are a splendid combination to begin a meal. So why not use a similar flavor pairing as a finale, as well? I serve this nutmeg-scented cantaloupe sherbet accompanied by crunchy caramel tuiles with tiny flecks of bacon in them. I first developed the sherbet after the late M.F.K. Fisher told me her father put nutmeg on his melon. Tiny shards of crunchy bacon dot the yummy, lacy caramel cookies. You can make them ahead and store them in an airtight container, but don't refrigerate them, because they'll become soggy.

MAKE THE SHERBET:

1. Purée the cantaloupe in a food processor. There should be about 2½–3 cups purée. Add the lemon juice, sugar, salt, and nutmeg and process until smooth, about 30 seconds. Scrape the mixture into a large bowl and stir in the milk. Scrape the mixture into a metal container, such as a cake pan, cover, and freeze until almost solid, at least 4 hours.

2. About an hour before serving, cut the frozen sherbet into cubes and put them in the processor. Begin by pulsing and then process until the sherbet is very smooth and light in color. Serve at once for a softer consistency, or return it to the freezer for about 1 hour. The sherbet may be reprocessed if serving it on a second or third occasion. Serve in small scoops with a light dusting of freshly grated nutmeg on top, accompanied by bacon tuiles.

FOR THE CARAMEL BACON TUILES:

Unsalted butter to grease cookie sheets

4 tablespoons unsalted butter

¼ cup light corn syrup

⅓ cup firmly packed light brown sugar

¼ teaspoon ground ginger

½ tablespoon brandy

½ cup flour

2 slices bacon, cooked until crisp, blotted on paper towels, and minced

MAKE THE CARAMEL BACON TUILES:

3. Preheat your oven to 350°F. Butter 2 cookie sheets.

4. Combine the remaining 4 tablespoons butter, corn syrup, brown sugar, ginger, and brandy in a small saucepan. Bring to a boil over medium heat, stir in the flour, and cook for 1 minute. Remove from heat, stir in the bacon, and cool for 1 minute.

5. Drop the batter by generous rounded teaspoonfuls onto the buttered cookie sheets. This recipe will make 16 large cookies. They will measure 2½ inches in diameter once they flatten, so only bake about 4 at a time. Bake in the middle of the oven for 8–9 minutes, or until dark golden.

6. Remove the pan from the oven and let the cookies cool on a cookie sheet for 1–2 minutes to firm slightly, then lift them off one at a time with a metal spatula. Wrap each cookie around a rolling pin or straight-sided glass and let them cool, then remove and set aside until all cookies are baked. If the cookies become too crisp to handle, return the pan to the oven for a few seconds. Continue until all the tuiles are cooked.

Suppliers of
Fine Specialty Bacons

BACON OF THE MONTH CLUB, Oxnard, CA; 888-472-5283; *www.gratefulpalate.com*. In two years, BOMC has grown from 1,000 to 2,100 customers and sells 40 different bacons.

BENTON'S COUNTRY HAMS, North Madisonville, TN; 423-442-5003; *www.bentonscountryhams.com*. Salt-cured Virginia slab bacon.

BROADBENT'S B&B FOOD PRODUCTS, Cadiz, KY; 800-841-2202; *www.broadbenthams.com*. Hickory-smoked peppered bacon and maplewood smoked bacon.

DA BECCA NATURAL FOODS, Clifton, TX; 800-793-6207. No-nitrate bacon made with no hormones or antibiotics.

D'ARTAGNAN, Newark, NJ; 800-327-8246; *www.dartagnan.com*. Wild boar and duck bacon, all Niman Ranch products, and foie gras.

S. WALLACE EDWARDS, Surry, VA; 757-294-3688. Hickory-smoked bacon, peppered bacon, brown sugar–cured bacon.

R. M. FELTS PACKING CO., Ivor, VA; 888-300-0971. Dry-cured country bacon, hams.

GATTON FARMS, Father's Country Hams, Bremen, KY; 270-525-3554; *www.fatherscountryham.com*. Dry-cured bacon with intense tastes.

HAM I AM!; 800-742-6426; *www.hamiam.com*. Hickory-smoked and peppered slab.

JANSAL VALLEY, Sid Wainer & Son, New Bedford, MA; 800-423-8333; *www.sidwainer.com*. Applewood- and corncob-smoked New Hampshire bacon.

KUNZLER & CO., Lancaster, PA; 888-586-9537; *www.kunzler.com*. Pennsylvania's Amish country-hardwood-smoked bacons, peppered and lower-fat variations.

LAZY H SMOKEHOUSE, Kirbyville, TX; 409-423-3309. Velma Willett's old-fashioned smokehouse; no artificial heat, preservatives, or MSG. Very smoky.

McARTHUR'S SMOKEHOUSE, Charlottesville, VA; 800-382-8177; *www.mcarthurssmokehouse.com*. Applewood-smoked bacon; hickory-smoked products since 1876, all mail order.

MEACHAM COUNTRY HAMS, Sturgis, KY; 800-552-3190; *www.meachamhams.com*. Since 1932, a full line of bacon, hams, and sausages.

NEW BRAUNFELS SMOKEHOUSE, New Braunfels, TX; 830-625-9138; *www.nbsmokehouse.com*. Slow-cured, hickory-smoked bacon from Texas smokers.

NIMAN RANCH, Oakland, CA; 866-808-0340; *www.nimanranch.com*. All-natural, hormone-free meat products from 300 independent family farmers whose animals are treated humanely, fed all-natural feeds, and allowed to mature naturally. Their bacon is sublime.

NODINE'S SMOKEHOUSE, Torrington, CT; 800-222-2059; *www.nodinesmokehouse.com*. Started in 1969, their bacon is featured in all major New York stores.

NORTH COUNTRY SMOKEHOUSE, Claremont, NH; 800-258-4304; *www.ncsmokehouse.com*. Family-run since 1912, with a full line of apple- and cob-smoked bacons, peppered bacon, and Canadian bacon stick.

NUESKE'S, Wittenberg, WI; 800-392-2266; *www.nueskes.com*. Many connoisseurs' favorite bacon.

OSCAR'S BACON, Warrensburg, NY; 800-627-3431; *www.oscarssmokedmeats.com*. Canadian, British, Irish, Cajun, Texas, and more. Chemical-free, salt-and-honey-cured.

THE REAL CANADIAN BACON CO., Troy, MI; 866-222-6601; *www.realcanadianbacon.com*. Imports lean, smokeless pea-meal bacon from Canada.

R. W. HOBBS, Richmond, CA; 510-232-5577. Applewood-smoked "California style" bacon, pancetta.

SALUMERIA BIELLESE, New York, NY; *www.salumeriabiellese.com*. Since 1925. the smallest USDA-approved meat packer in the U.S. Applewood-smoked bacon, guanciale, pancetta, and pepato-salted pancetta made with herbs and olive oil and pressed between granite slabs.

SUMMERFIELD FARM, Culpepper, VA; 800-898-3276; *www.summerfieldfarm.com*. Jamie Nicoll's molasses and brown-sugar-cured slab bacon is like Christmas pudding, says chef Tom Colicchio.

S. WALLACE EDWARDS & SONS, Surry, VA; 800-222-4267. In its 81st year of preparing all-natural smoked and brown-sugar-cured bacon.

THE SWISS MEAT AND SAUSAGE CO., Swiss, MO; 800-793-SWISS; *www.swissmeats@ktis.net*. Hickory- or applewood-smoked, sugar- or honey-cured, as well as cottage and pepper bacons.

VERMONT SMOKE & CURE, South Barre, VT; 1-802-476-4666. Smokehouse with the social mission of promoting the economic vitality of local family farms by creating an ever-growing network of local suppliers from which it buys meats to sell under its label. Specialties include: maple-cured and cob-smoked bacon.

WILLIAM'S BRITISH STYLE MEATS, Lumberton, NC; 910-608-2226; *www.britishbacon.com*. Irish- and English-style bacon and other pork products cured and smoked.

Index